Revealing Lake Garda : A Travel

Preparation Guide

Marcus Nwolu

All rights reserved. No part of this publication may be reproduced, distributed, or transmitted in any form or by any means, including photocopying, recording, or other electronic or mechanical methods, without the prior written permission of the publisher, except in the case of brief quotations embodied in critical reviews and certain other noncommercial uses permitted by copyright law.

Copyright © (Marcus Nwolu) (2024).

Revealing Lake Garda :A Travel	**1**
Preparation Guide	**1**
Marcus Nwolu	**1**
Introduction	**7**
CHAPTER ONE	**9**
- Overview of Lake Garda	9
- Geography and Location	13
- Climate and Best Time to Visit	16
CHAPTER TWO	**19**
Getting to Lake Garda	19
- Transportation Options	19
- Renting Cars or Bicycles	26
CHAPTER THREE	**31**
Exploring the Towns around Lake Garda	31
- Desenzano del Garda	31
- Sirmione	37
- Bardolino	40
- Lazise	44
- Malcesine	48
- Riva del Garda	51
CHAPTER FOUR	**57**
Activities at Lake Garda	57
- Water Sports: Sailing, Windsurfing, Kitesurfing 57	
- Hiking and Trekking Trails	59
- Cycling Routes	61
- Golfing	65
- Spa and Wellness Centers	69
CHAPTER FIVE	**73**

Cultural and Historical Attractions	73
- Scaliger Castle in Sirmione	73
- Grotte di Catullo in Sirmione	77
- Vittoriale degli Italiani in Gardone Riviera	80
- Rocca Scaligera in Malcesine	83
- Roman Ruins in Desenzano del Garda	85

CHAPTER SIX — **91**

Culinary Delights of Lake Garda	91
- Traditional Dishes and Local Cuisine	91
- Wine Tasting Tours	94
- Olive Oil Tasting	95

CHAPTER SEVEN — **99**

Shopping and Markets	99
- Local Markets	99
- Boutique Shops	102
- Souvenirs and Handicrafts	105

CHAPTER EIGHT — **109**

Practical Information	109
- Currency and Banking	109
- Language	115
- Safety Tips	117

CHAPTER NINE — **121**

Accommodation Options	121
- Hotels	121
- Bed and Breakfasts	124
- Campsites	129
- Rental Apartments and Villas	133

CHAPTER TEN — **137**

Day Trips and Excursions	137

- Verona	137
- Venice	143
- Milan	149

CHAPTER ELEVEN — **153**
Insider Tips and Recommendations — 153
- Hidden Gems — 153
- Off-the-Beaten-Path Spots — 156
- Budget-Friendly Activities — 159

CHAPTER TWELE — **163**
Conclusion — 163

Introduction

Welcome to Lake Garda, a slice of paradise nestled in the heart of northern Italy. As I stand on the shores of this majestic lake, surrounded by the towering peaks of the Italian Alps, I can't help but be captivated by its beauty. From its crystal-clear waters to its charming lakeside villages, Lake Garda is a destination like no other.

In this comprehensive travel guide, I invite you to join me on a journey of discovery as we explore everything this enchanting region has to offer. Whether you're seeking relaxation, adventure, or simply a taste of la dolce vita, Lake Garda has something for everyone.

From the bustling streets of Desenzano del Garda to the serene shores of Sirmione, each town along the lake has its own unique charm and character waiting to be explored. Sample delicious Italian cuisine, sip on world-class wines, or simply soak up the sun as you wander through the picturesque streets lined with colorful buildings and quaint cafes.

But Lake Garda isn't just about its towns and villages – it's also a playground for outdoor enthusiasts. With its mild climate and diverse landscape, the lake offers a plethora of activities for visitors of all ages. Whether you're into hiking, cycling, water sports, or simply relaxing on the beach, you'll find endless opportunities to indulge your sense of adventure.

And let's not forget about the rich history and culture that permeates every corner of Lake Garda. From ancient Roman ruins to medieval castles, the region is steeped in history, just waiting to be uncovered. Take a step back in time as you explore the historic landmarks and archaeological sites that dot the landscape, and immerse yourself in the fascinating stories of the past.

But perhaps the greatest allure of Lake Garda lies in its natural beauty. With its shimmering blue waters, verdant hillsides, and dramatic mountain backdrops, it's easy to see why this enchanting destination has captured the hearts of travelers for centuries. Whether you're admiring the sunset from the shores of Gardone Riviera or taking a leisurely boat ride across the lake, the beauty of Lake Garda is sure to leave you spellbound.

So come along with me as we embark on an unforgettable journey to Lake Garda. Whether you're a first-time visitor or a seasoned traveler, there's always something new to discover in this idyllic corner of Italy. So pack your bags, grab your camera, and get ready to experience the magic of Lake Garda – I promise you won't be disappointed.

CHAPTER ONE

- Overview of Lake Garda

Welcome to Lake Garda, Italy's largest lake, nestled in the picturesque region of northern Italy. As your guide, I'll lead you through the wonders of this stunning destination, renowned for its breathtaking landscapes, charming towns, and rich cultural heritage. Join me as we embark on an unforgettable journey around the enchanting shores of Lake Garda.

Introduction to Lake Garda

Stretching over 50 kilometers in length and spanning three provinces (Verona, Brescia, and Trento), Lake Garda captivates visitors with its crystal-clear waters, lush greenery, and towering mountains. Its diverse landscape offers a myriad of opportunities for outdoor adventures, cultural exploration, and relaxation.

Getting There

Whether you're arriving by car, train, or plane, Lake Garda is easily accessible from major cities like Milan, Venice, and Verona. The closest airports are Verona Villafranca Airport (VRN) and Bergamo Orio al Serio Airport (BGY), both of which offer convenient connections to the lake.

Where to Stay

From luxury resorts to cozy bed and breakfasts, Lake Garda offers a wide range of accommodation options to suit every budget and preference. For a touch of elegance, consider staying at the iconic Grand Hotel Fasano or the historic Villa Cortine Palace Hotel in Sirmione. Alternatively, immerse yourself in the local culture by renting a charming lakeside apartment or villa in towns like Malcesine or Bardolino.

Exploring the Towns and Villages

Each town and village around Lake Garda has its own unique charm and attractions waiting to be discovered. Begin your journey in Sirmione, known for its medieval castle and thermal baths. Stroll along the cobblestone streets of Lazise and Peschiera del Garda, where colorful buildings and bustling markets create a lively atmosphere. Don't miss the opportunity to visit picturesque Malcesine, home to the iconic Scaliger Castle and a gateway to Mount Baldo.

Outdoor Adventures

With its stunning natural scenery and temperate climate, Lake Garda is a paradise for outdoor enthusiasts. Spend your days hiking through the rugged mountains, cycling along scenic trails, or sailing across the sparkling waters. Thrill-seekers can try their hand at windsurfing, kiteboarding, or paragliding, while those seeking tranquility can relax on the sun-kissed beaches or indulge in a leisurely boat cruise.

Cultural Delights

Immerse yourself in Lake Garda's rich cultural heritage by exploring its historic landmarks, museums, and artistic treasures. Marvel at the Roman ruins of Grotte di Catullo in Sirmione, admire the frescoes of the Scaliger Castle in Malcesine, or wander through the charming streets of Gardone Riviera, home to the eclectic Vittoriale degli Italiani estate. Don't forget to sample the region's culinary delights, from fresh seafood and traditional risotto to world-class wines like Bardolino and Lugana.

Events and Festivals

Throughout the year, Lake Garda comes alive with a vibrant calendar of events and festivals celebrating its history, culture, and traditions. Join the festivities during the annual Verona Opera

Festival, held in the historic Arena di Verona, or experience the colorful Carnival celebrations in towns like Riva del Garda and Desenzano del Garda. For wine enthusiasts, the Bardolino Chiaretto Pink Night offers the perfect opportunity to taste the region's finest rosé wines against the backdrop of a stunning sunset.

Practical Tips

Before you embark on your Lake Garda adventure, here are a few practical tips to ensure a smooth and enjoyable trip:

1. Weather: Lake Garda enjoys a Mediterranean climate, with mild winters and warm summers. Be sure to check the weather forecast before your trip and pack accordingly.
2. Transportation: While renting a car offers flexibility for exploring the region, public transportation options such as buses and ferries are also available for getting around.
3. Language: Italian is the primary language spoken in Lake Garda, although English is widely understood, especially in tourist areas.
4. Currency:The official currency in Italy is the Euro (EUR). Be sure to have some cash on hand for small purchases, as not all establishments accept credit cards.
5. Reservations: During peak tourist season (June to August), it's advisable to make reservations for

accommodations, restaurants, and activities in advance to avoid disappointment.

- Geography and Location

As a first-time traveler to Lake Garda, exploring its geography and location was essential to fully appreciate the beauty and charm of this stunning destination. Situated in northern Italy, Lake Garda is the largest lake in the country, spanning approximately 370 square kilometers. Nestled between the provinces of Verona, Brescia, and Trento, Lake Garda boasts a diverse landscape characterized by crystal-clear waters, picturesque towns, and majestic mountains.

As I gazed out over the vast expanse of Lake Garda, I was captivated by its sheer beauty. The lake is surrounded by towering mountains to the north, including the dramatic peaks of the Dolomites and the Trentino Alps. These rugged mountains provide a breathtaking backdrop to the tranquil waters below, creating a scene of unparalleled natural beauty.

To the south, the landscape changes dramatically, giving way to rolling hills, olive groves, and vineyards. The mild climate of Lake Garda, influenced by its proximity to the Mediterranean Sea, makes it an ideal environment for the cultivation of olives, lemons, and grapes. As I explored the quaint villages and towns that dot the shoreline, I was struck by the vibrant colors of the countryside, from the lush greenery of the hillsides to the vibrant hues of the flowers that line the streets.

One of the most iconic features of Lake Garda is its crystal-clear waters, which shimmer in the sunlight like liquid sapphire. The lake is renowned for its clarity and purity, making it a haven for water sports enthusiasts and nature lovers alike. Whether you prefer swimming, sailing, windsurfing, or simply lounging on the shore, Lake Garda offers endless opportunities to immerse yourself in its pristine waters.

The towns and villages that line the shores of Lake Garda are steeped in history and charm, each with its own unique character and attractions. In the south, the town of Sirmione is renowned for its thermal baths and ancient Roman ruins, including the striking Scaliger Castle, which juts out into the lake on a narrow peninsula. Further north, the town of Malcesine is dominated by the imposing Scaliger Castle, which offers panoramic views of the lake and surrounding mountains from its towering ramparts.

As I traveled around the lake, I was struck by the diversity of its landscape and the warmth of its people. From the bustling promenades of Desenzano del Garda to the tranquil olive groves of Bardolino, each town offers its own unique blend of history, culture, and natural beauty. Whether you are exploring ancient ruins, sampling local wines, or simply soaking up the sun on the beach, Lake Garda has something to offer everyone.

In addition to its natural beauty, Lake Garda is also home to a wealth of cultural attractions and outdoor activities. The lake is surrounded by numerous hiking and biking trails, which meander through lush forests, verdant vineyards, and quaint villages. For those interested in history and culture, the region boasts a wealth of museums, galleries, and historical sites, including the Grottoes of Catullus in Sirmione and the Vittoriale degli Italiani in Gardone Riviera.

No visit to Lake Garda would be complete without sampling the region's culinary delights. From fresh seafood and traditional risotto to hearty polenta and delicate pastries, the cuisine of Lake Garda is as diverse as it is delicious. Many restaurants offer lakeside dining, allowing you to savor your meal against the backdrop of the shimmering waters and majestic mountains.

As the sun sets over Lake Garda, casting a golden glow across the water, I am filled with a sense of wonder and gratitude. This magical place, with its breathtaking beauty and warm hospitality, has captured my heart in a way that I never thought possible. Whether you are seeking adventure, relaxation, or simply a chance to reconnect with nature, Lake Garda truly offers something for everyone. So come, immerse yourself in the beauty of Italy's largest lake, and discover why Lake Garda is truly a treasure worth exploring.

- Climate and Best Time to Visit

Before embarking on any adventure, it's essential to understand the climate of the destination to ensure a comfortable and enjoyable experience. Lake Garda benefits from a mild Mediterranean climate, characterized by hot summers and relatively mild winters. However, due to its unique geographical location, the climate can vary slightly depending on the region around the lake.

Spring (March - May):
Spring heralds the awakening of nature around Lake Garda, with blossoming flowers, lush greenery, and pleasant temperatures. During this time, the weather is generally mild, making it ideal for outdoor activities such as hiking, cycling, and sightseeing. The crowds are relatively thinner

compared to the peak summer season, allowing for a more peaceful and authentic experience.

Summer (June - August):
Summer is undoubtedly the busiest time of year around Lake Garda, as tourists from all over the world flock to its shores to bask in the Mediterranean sunshine. With long, sunny days and temperatures ranging from warm to hot, it's the perfect time for swimming, sunbathing, and enjoying water sports such as sailing, windsurfing, and kayaking. However, be prepared for larger crowds and higher prices during this peak tourist season.

Autumn (September - November):
As summer transitions into autumn, Lake Garda takes on a magical quality, with the changing colors of the foliage painting the landscape in vibrant hues of red, orange, and gold. The weather remains pleasant, albeit slightly cooler than summer, making it an excellent time for outdoor activities and sightseeing. Autumn also brings harvest festivals and culinary delights, showcasing the region's rich gastronomic traditions.

Winter (December - February):
While not as popular as the warmer seasons, winter still holds its own charm around Lake Garda. The temperatures are cooler, and occasional snowfall dusts the surrounding mountains, creating a picturesque winter wonderland. Although some

tourist attractions may have reduced hours or be closed during this time, it's perfect for those seeking a peaceful retreat amidst the serenity of the lake.

Best Time to Visit:

Choosing the best time to visit Lake Garda depends on your personal preferences and interests. If you're a sun seeker looking to soak up the Mediterranean warmth and partake in water activities, then the summer months of June to August are ideal. However, if you prefer milder temperatures and fewer crowds, consider visiting during the shoulder seasons of spring or autumn. Additionally, winter offers a unique experience for those seeking tranquility and a slower pace of life.

CHAPTER TWO

Getting to Lake Garda

- Transportation Options

1. Getting to Lake Garda

Before diving into transportation within the region, let's talk about getting to Lake Garda itself. Depending on your starting point, there are several convenient options:

By Air: If you're traveling from afar, the closest airports to Lake Garda are Verona Airport (VRN) and Bergamo Orio al Serio Airport (BGY). Both airports offer domestic and international flights, with Verona being the closest to the lake.

By Train: Italy's efficient train network provides easy access to cities near Lake Garda, such as Verona and Brescia. From there, you can transfer to buses or taxis to reach your final destination.

By Car: Renting a car gives you the freedom to explore Lake Garda at your own pace. Major highways connect the region to nearby cities, and once you arrive, navigating the lake's scenic roads is a delight.

2. Getting Around Lake Garda

Once you've arrived at Lake Garda, you'll find a variety of transportation options to help you explore its charming towns, breathtaking landscapes, and cultural attractions.

Public Buses: The local bus network is a convenient and affordable way to travel between towns along the lake. Schedules are frequent, especially during the peak tourist season, and routes cover most areas of interest. Keep in mind that buses can get crowded during peak times, so plan accordingly.

Ferries and Boats: One of the best ways to experience the beauty of Lake Garda is by taking a ferry or boat ride. The lake's crystal-clear waters and scenic coastline make for unforgettable journeys between towns such as Sirmione, Malcesine, and Riva del Garda. Ferry services operate year-round, with increased frequency during the summer months.

Cycling: For the adventurous traveler, cycling is a fantastic way to explore Lake Garda and its surroundings. The region offers a network of well-maintained cycling paths that wind through vineyards, olive groves, and charming villages.

Renting a bike is easy, and many hotels and shops offer rental services.

Car Rental: While public transportation and boats are convenient for getting around Lake Garda, renting a car provides flexibility and access to off-the-beaten-path destinations. With your own vehicle, you can explore hidden gems, visit wineries, and enjoy scenic drives along the lake's shores.

3. Day Trips and Excursions

In addition to exploring the towns and attractions around Lake Garda, consider taking day trips to nearby destinations that offer unique cultural experiences and natural wonders.

Verona: Just a short distance from Lake Garda, the historic city of Verona beckons with its ancient Roman ruins, charming piazzas, and iconic Juliet's balcony. Don't miss the opportunity to explore this UNESCO World Heritage Site and immerse yourself in its rich history and culture.

Venice: While Venice is further away from Lake Garda, it's worth the journey for a day trip to this iconic city of canals and bridges. Marvel at the grandeur of St. Mark's Square, take a gondola ride along the waterways, and discover hidden gems in the narrow streets of the city.

Trento and the Dolomites: To the north of Lake Garda lies the majestic region of Trentino-Alto Adige, home to the Dolomite Mountains and the charming city of Trento. Explore alpine landscapes, visit historic castles, and indulge in delicious local cuisine in this scenic corner of Italy.

4. Practical Tips for Transportation

As you plan your transportation around Lake Garda, here are some practical tips to keep in mind:

Check Schedules: Be sure to check the schedules for buses, ferries, and other modes of transportation, especially if you're traveling during the off-peak season when services may be less frequent.

Purchase Tickets in Advance:For popular ferry routes and attractions, consider purchasing tickets in advance to avoid long lines and ensure availability, especially during peak tourist season.

Pack Light: If you're planning to use public transportation, keep in mind that space may be limited, especially during busy times. Pack light and consider bringing a daypack for essentials.

Be Mindful of Timings:Public transportation schedules may vary, so plan your journeys accordingly, especially if you have time-sensitive activities or connections.

Stay Informed: Stay updated on any changes or disruptions to transportation services by checking official websites, local news sources, or consulting with your accommodation provider.

- Nearest Airports and Train Stations

Arriving by Air:
Lake Garda is conveniently located within reach of several major airports, providing international travelers with various options for reaching this breathtaking destination. Depending on your itinerary and preferences, you can choose from the following airports:

1. Verona Airport (Valerio Catullo Airport - VRN):
   - Distance from Lake Garda: Approximately 15 kilometers (9 miles) to the city of Verona, which is situated on the southeastern shore of Lake Garda.
   - Verona Airport serves as the primary gateway for travelers heading to Lake Garda. It offers domestic and international flights, connecting the region to major cities across Europe and beyond.
   - From Verona Airport, you can easily reach Lake Garda by car, taxi, or shuttle service. The journey typically takes around 30 to 45 minutes, depending on your final destination along the lake.

2. Bergamo Airport (Orio al Serio International Airport - BGY):

- Distance from Lake Garda: Approximately 100 kilometers (62 miles) to the east of Lake Garda.

- While Bergamo Airport is not as close as Verona Airport, it remains a viable option for travelers seeking budget-friendly flights and additional airline choices.

- From Bergamo Airport, you can reach Lake Garda by rental car, shuttle service, or a combination of bus and train travel. The journey usually takes around 1.5 to 2 hours, depending on traffic and transportation connections.

3. Milan Airports (Milan Malpensa Airport - MXP and Milan Linate Airport - LIN):

- Distance from Lake Garda: Approximately 150 to 180 kilometers (93 to 112 miles) to the west of Lake Garda.

- While Milan's airports are further away from Lake Garda compared to Verona and Bergamo, they offer extensive international connections and flight options.

- Travelers arriving at Milan Malpensa or Milan Linate can access Lake Garda by rental car, shuttle service, or a combination of train and bus travel. The journey typically takes around 2 to 3 hours, depending on transportation choices and traffic conditions.

Arriving by Train:

For travelers opting to explore Lake Garda via train, the region is accessible via several nearby railway stations. While Lake Garda itself does not have a train station directly on its shores, the following stations serve as convenient entry points for rail travelers:

1. Desenzano del Garda-Sirmione Train Station:
   - Located on the southwestern shore of Lake Garda, Desenzano del Garda-Sirmione Train Station is one of the busiest railway hubs in the region.
   - The station offers regular train services connecting major cities such as Milan, Verona, Venice, and Brescia, making it a convenient option for travelers arriving from different parts of Italy and beyond.
   - From Desenzano del Garda-Sirmione Train Station, visitors can easily access Lake Garda's lakeside towns and resorts via taxi, bus, or ferry services.

2. Peschiera del Garda Train Station:
   - Situated on the southeastern shore of Lake Garda, Peschiera del Garda Train Station serves as another key transportation hub in the area.
   - The station provides connections to various destinations across Italy, including Verona, Milan, Venice, and Brescia, via regional and intercity train services.
   - Travelers arriving at Peschiera del Garda Train Station can continue their journey to Lake Garda's nearby towns and attractions by taxi, bus, or ferry, depending on their final destination.

3. Verona Porta Nuova Train Station:

   - While not directly on the shores of Lake Garda, Verona Porta Nuova Train Station serves as a major railway hub in the region, offering connections to destinations throughout Italy and beyond.

   - From Verona Porta Nuova Train Station, travelers can take regional trains to nearby towns such as Desenzano del Garda and Peschiera del Garda, both of which provide access to Lake Garda via additional transportation options.

   - Verona Porta Nuova Train Station also offers convenient connections to Verona Airport, making it an ideal choice for travelers combining air and rail travel.

- Renting Cars or Bicycles

Renting Cars: Freedom on Wheels

There's something undeniably liberating about hitting the open road with nothing but the horizon stretching out before you. Renting a car offers unparalleled freedom, allowing you to explore every corner of Lake Garda at your own pace. Whether you're craving the cobblestone streets of charming villages or the winding roads that hug the shoreline, a car provides the ultimate flexibility to go wherever your heart desires.

One of the biggest advantages of renting a car is the convenience it offers. With your own wheels, you're not beholden to the schedules of public transportation or the constraints of tour groups. Want to catch a sunrise over the lake or linger in a quaint trattoria until the wee hours of the morning? With a car at your disposal, the choice is entirely yours.

Additionally, renting a car opens up a world of possibilities beyond Lake Garda itself. With the freedom to venture further afield, you can explore nearby attractions such as the medieval town of Sirmione, the vineyards of Valpolicella, or the historic city of Verona, immortalized by Shakespeare's Romeo and Juliet.

However, with great freedom comes great responsibility, and there are certainly some drawbacks to consider when opting for four wheels over two. Chief among these is the challenge of navigating Lake Garda's narrow streets and limited parking options, particularly during the peak tourist season. Additionally, renting a car can be costly, especially when factoring in fuel, insurance, and potential tolls.

Renting Bicycles: Embracing a Slower Pace

For those who prefer to take life at a more leisurely pace, renting a bicycle offers a delightful alternative to the hustle and bustle of motorized transportation. There's something inherently romantic about the idea of pedaling along Lake Garda's sun-dappled shores, with the gentle breeze in your hair and the scent of olive groves wafting through the air.

One of the biggest advantages of renting a bicycle is the opportunity it provides to truly immerse yourself in the stunning natural beauty of Lake Garda. From the lush vineyards of Bardolino to the rugged cliffs of Limone sul Garda, cycling allows you to experience the landscape up close and personal, stopping whenever the mood strikes to snap a photo or simply soak in the scenery.

Moreover, cycling is not only good for the soul but also for the body. Lake Garda boasts a network of scenic cycle paths that cater to cyclists of all skill levels, from leisurely waterfront promenades to challenging mountain trails. Whether you're a seasoned cyclist or a casual rider, exploring Lake Garda by bike offers a unique opportunity to stay active while indulging in some much-needed relaxation.

However, it's important to acknowledge that cycling may not be suitable for everyone or every occasion. While Lake Garda is generally bike-friendly, some areas may be hilly or inaccessible by bike, requiring a certain level of physical fitness and endurance. Additionally, the pace of travel is inherently slower when cycling, which may not be ideal for those with limited time or a packed itinerary.

Making the Choice: Finding the Right Balance

As I weighed the pros and cons of renting a car versus renting a bicycle, I realized that there is no one-size-fits-all answer. Ultimately, the best choice depends on a variety of factors, including personal preferences, travel style, and the specific experiences I hope to gain from my time at Lake Garda.

For those seeking freedom and flexibility, renting a car may be the ideal option, providing the means to explore the region's diverse landscapes and attractions at their own pace. On the other hand, those craving a more intimate connection with nature and a slower pace of travel may find that renting a bicycle allows them to fully immerse themselves in the beauty of Lake Garda.

CHAPTER THREE

Exploring the Towns around Lake Garda

- Desenzano del Garda

As I embarked on my journey to explore the enchanting region of Lake Garda, I found myself drawn to the picturesque town of Desenzano del Garda. Nestled on the southern shore of Italy's largest lake, Desenzano exudes a timeless charm that captivates visitors with its stunning vistas, rich history, and vibrant culture. Join me as I delve into the wonders of this hidden gem, weaving together practical travel tips, historical insights, and personal experiences to create the ultimate Lake Garda travel guide.

Introduction to Desenzano del Garda

As I arrived in Desenzano del Garda, I was immediately struck by the town's idyllic setting against the backdrop of shimmering blue waters and rolling hills. Renowned for its Mediterranean climate and breathtaking landscapes, Lake Garda servesX DE as a playground for outdoor enthusiasts and a haven for those seeking tranquility amidst nature's beauty.

Desenzano, with its labyrinthine streets, charming piazzas, and historic landmarks, embodies the essence of Italian hospitality and warmth. Whether strolling along the promenade, savoring local delicacies at trattorias, or exploring ancient ruins, every corner of Desenzano beckons with the promise of discovery and adventure.

Getting to Desenzano del Garda

For travelers arriving by air, the closest airports to Desenzano del Garda are Verona Villafranca Airport (VRN) and Milan Bergamo Airport (BGY), both of which offer convenient access to the town via public transportation or rental car. From Verona, a scenic drive along the eastern shore of Lake Garda leads directly to Desenzano, while Milan Bergamo provides easy connections via train or bus.

Alternatively, those traveling by train can reach Desenzano via the efficient Italian rail network, with frequent services from major cities such as Milan, Venice, and Florence. Upon arrival at Desenzano's train station, taxis and local buses are readily available to transport visitors to their accommodations or desired destinations within the town.

Accommodations in Desenzano del Garda

Desenzano del Garda boasts a diverse range of accommodations to suit every budget and preference, from luxurious waterfront resorts to cozy bed and breakfasts nestled within the historic center. During my stay, I opted for a charming boutique hotel overlooking the lake, where I was greeted with personalized service and panoramic views that took my breath away.

For travelers seeking a more immersive experience, agriturismi (farm stays) offer an authentic taste of rural life amidst the vineyards and olive groves that dot the countryside surrounding Desenzano. These family-run establishments provide cozy accommodations, home-cooked meals made from fresh local ingredients, and opportunities to participate in agricultural activities such as grape harvesting and olive picking.

Exploring Desenzano del Garda

With its wealth of historical and cultural attractions, Desenzano del Garda offers endless opportunities for exploration and discovery. One of the town's most iconic landmarks is the imposing Scaliger Castle, perched atop a rocky promontory overlooking the lake. Dating back to the 10th century, this medieval fortress offers commanding views of Desenzano and the surrounding countryside, making it a must-visit destination for history enthusiasts and photographers alike.

As I wandered through the cobblestone streets of Desenzano's historic center, I was enchanted by its charming architecture, bustling markets, and vibrant atmosphere. The Piazza Malvezzi, with its elegant arcades and outdoor cafes, serves as the heart of the town, providing the perfect spot to relax and soak in the ambiance while sipping a cappuccino or enjoying a gelato.

For a glimpse into Desenzano's rich maritime heritage, a visit to the Museo Civico Archeologico is highly recommended. Housed within a former monastery, this museum showcases an impressive collection of artifacts ranging from Roman pottery and sculptures to ancient navigational instruments, offering insight into the town's role as a strategic port and trading hub throughout the centuries.

Outdoor Activities in Desenzano del Garda

As an avid lover of the outdoors, I was thrilled to discover the wealth of recreational opportunities that await visitors to Desenzano del Garda. Whether sailing across the azure waters of Lake Garda, hiking through scenic nature trails, or cycling along the picturesque coastline, there's no shortage of ways to immerse oneself in the natural beauty of the region.

One of the highlights of my trip was a leisurely boat excursion to the nearby Isola del Garda, the largest island on Lake Garda and home to a magnificent

Venetian-style villa surrounded by lush gardens and olive groves. Guided tours of the villa and grounds offer a fascinating glimpse into the island's storied past, while panoramic views of the lake provide a perfect backdrop for relaxation and reflection.

For those seeking adrenaline-fueled thrills, Desenzano del Garda is also a paradise for water sports enthusiasts, with opportunities for windsurfing, kiteboarding, and jet skiing abound. The town's sandy beaches, such as Spiaggia d'Oro and Spiaggia Desenzanino, provide ideal settings for sunbathing, swimming, and indulging in the simple pleasures of la dolce vita.

Culinary Delights of Desenzano del Garda

No visit to Desenzano del Garda would be complete without savoring the delectable flavors of Lombard cuisine, characterized by its emphasis on fresh, locally sourced ingredients and simple yet elegant preparations. From traditional trattorias to Michelin-starred restaurants, the town offers a diverse array of dining options to suit every palate and budget.

One of my most memorable dining experiences in Desenzano was a leisurely lunch at a rustic osteria overlooking the lake, where I indulged in a feast of regional specialties such as risotto al nero di seppia (squid ink risotto), baccalà alla gardesana (salted cod with polenta), and torta delle rose (rose-shaped cake) for dessert. Each dish was a celebration of the region's culinary heritage, expertly prepared and served with warmth and hospitality.

For wine enthusiasts, Desenzano del Garda is also a gateway to the renowned wine-producing regions of Lombardy and Veneto, where vineyards thrive in the fertile soil and Mediterranean climate. Guided wine tours and tastings offer the opportunity to sample a diverse selection of varietals, from crisp whites such as Lugana and Trebbiano to robust reds like Valpolicella and Bardolino, all while learning about the history and traditions of winemaking in the area.

Day Trips from Desenzano del Garda

While Desenzano del Garda offers more than enough attractions to fill an itinerary, the town's strategic location makes it an ideal base for exploring the wider Lake Garda region and beyond. From charming lakeside villages to historic cities and natural wonders, there's no shortage of day trip options to suit every interest and inclination.

One popular excursion is a visit to the nearby town of Sirmione, renowned for its thermal baths, medieval castle, and picturesque old town. A leisurely stroll along the town's cobblestone streets leads to the Scaliger Castle, where panoramic views of Lake Garda and the surrounding countryside await. Afterward, a dip in the healing waters of the Terme di Sirmione offers the perfect opportunity to unwind and rejuvenate body and soul.

- Sirmione

Sirmione, a gem nestled on the southern shore of Lake Garda, Italy, is a place of mesmerizing beauty and historical significance. As I embarked on this journey to explore Sirmione and its surroundings, I was filled with anticipation and wonder, eager to uncover its hidden treasures and immerse myself in its rich history and stunning natural landscapes.

Arrival in Sirmione:
As I arrived in Sirmione, I was immediately struck by the town's timeless charm and idyllic setting. The quaint streets lined with pastel-colored houses, the scent of blooming flowers lingering in the air, and the gentle breeze from the lake create a sense of tranquility that is simply enchanting. I can't help but feel like I've stepped into a postcard-perfect paradise.

Exploring the Historic Center:
Wandering through the historic center of Sirmione, I was transported back in time to a bygone era. The medieval architecture, cobblestone streets, and

ancient ruins tell stories of centuries past, offering a glimpse into the town's rich heritage. One of the highlights of the historic center is the Scaliger Castle, a 13th-century fortress that once served as a strategic stronghold against invaders. Climbing to the top of the castle's tower, I am rewarded with panoramic views of Lake Garda and the surrounding countryside, a sight that takes my breath away.

Relaxation at the Thermal Baths:
After a morning of exploration, I decided to indulge in some well-deserved relaxation at the thermal baths of Sirmione. Known for their healing properties and therapeutic benefits, the thermal waters of Sirmione have been revered since ancient times. As I soaked in the warm, mineral-rich waters, I feel my worries melt away, leaving me feeling rejuvenated and revitalized. It's the perfect way to unwind and pamper myself amidst the beauty of Lake Garda.

Cuisine and Culinary Delights:
No visit to Sirmione would be complete without sampling the region's delectable cuisine. From fresh seafood caught in the waters of Lake Garda to homemade pasta dishes bursting with flavor, Sirmione offers a culinary experience that is sure to delight even the most discerning palate. I found myself indulging in local specialties such as risotto al nero di seppia (squid ink risotto) and tortellini di zucca (pumpkin-filled pasta), accompanied by a

glass of crisp, refreshing Lugana wine. Each bite is a symphony of flavors, a true celebration of the rich culinary heritage of the region.

Leisure Activities and Outdoor Adventures:
For those seeking adventure and excitement, Sirmione offers a wealth of outdoor activities to suit every taste. From hiking and cycling along the shores of Lake Garda to sailing and windsurfing on its pristine waters, there's no shortage of ways to get active and explore the natural beauty of the area. For a more leisurely experience, I opt for a scenic boat cruise around the lake, taking in the breathtaking views of the surrounding mountains and charming lakeside villages. It's a truly unforgettable experience that allows me to appreciate the splendor of Lake Garda from a different perspective.

Day Trips and Excursions:
While Sirmione itself is a destination worthy of exploration, the surrounding area offers a plethora of day trip options for those looking to venture further afield. One popular excursion is a visit to the nearby town of Desenzano del Garda, known for its bustling piazzas, vibrant markets, and lively atmosphere. Another must-see attraction is the picturesque town of Garda, located on the eastern shore of Lake Garda, where visitors can stroll along the waterfront promenade, visit the quaint churches, and sample local delicacies at charming cafes and trattorias.

- Bardolino

As I take a leisurely stroll along the shores of Lake Garda, my senses are overwhelmed by the breathtaking beauty of this enchanting destination. Among the myriad of charming towns that dot the lake's shoreline, Bardolino stands out as a true gem, offering a perfect blend of natural splendor, cultural richness, and gastronomic delights. Join me on an immersive journey as we explore the wonders of Bardolino and uncover its hidden treasures in this comprehensive Lake Garda travel guide.

Introduction to Bardolino

Nestled on the eastern shores of Lake Garda in the Veneto region of northern Italy, Bardolino exudes an undeniable allure that captivates visitors from around the globe. Renowned for its picturesque waterfront, historic landmarks, and world-class vineyards, this charming town embodies the essence of la dolce vita.

Getting to Bardolino

Before diving into the heart of Bardolino, let's discuss the various transportation options available for travelers. For those arriving by air, the nearest airports are Verona Villafranca Airport (VRN) and Milan Bergamo Airport (BGY), both of which offer convenient access to Bardolino via taxi, shuttle, or rental car. Additionally, train services connect nearby cities like Verona and Desenzano del Garda to Bardolino, providing an efficient mode of transportation for those exploring the region by rail.

Accommodation in Bardolino

Bardolino boasts a diverse range of accommodation options to suit every traveler's preferences and budget. From luxurious lakeside resorts and boutique hotels to cozy bed and breakfasts and self-catering apartments, there's no shortage of choices for where to stay in Bardolino. For a truly immersive experience, consider booking a room with panoramic views of Lake Garda, allowing you to wake up to the soothing sounds of the water and bask in the scenic beauty of the surrounding landscape.

Exploring Bardolino

With its narrow cobblestone streets, historic piazzas, and charming waterfront promenade, Bardolino beckons visitors to wander and discover its many delights. Begin your exploration by meandering through the town center, where you'll encounter quaint shops selling local crafts, artisanal goods, and of course, bottles of Bardolino wine. Don't miss the opportunity to visit the Chiesa di San Severo, a beautiful church dating back to the 12th century, and the Museo del Vino Bardolino, where you can learn about the region's winemaking traditions through interactive exhibits and tastings.

Wine Tasting in Bardolino

No visit to Bardolino would be complete without indulging in a wine tasting experience at one of the area's renowned vineyards. With its mild climate and fertile soil, Bardolino is celebrated for producing high-quality wines, particularly the light and fruity Bardolino Chiaretto and the robust Bardolino Classico. Embark on a guided tour of a local winery, where you'll have the opportunity to stroll through vineyards, learn about the winemaking process, and sample a selection of exquisite wines paired with delicious regional specialties.

Culinary Delights of Bardolino

Bardolino's culinary scene is a gastronomic paradise, offering a tantalizing array of traditional dishes and gourmet delights to satisfy every palate. Indulge in fresh seafood delicacies at waterfront trattorias, savor authentic Italian pizza baked in wood-fired ovens, and treat yourself to creamy gelato in a rainbow of flavors. For a true taste of Bardolino, be sure to sample local specialties such as risotto al tastasal, a savory rice dish flavored with pork sausage, and torta di mele, a delectable apple cake that pairs perfectly with a glass of Bardolino wine.

Outdoor Activities in Bardolino

For outdoor enthusiasts, Bardolino provides a playground of recreational opportunities amidst its stunning natural surroundings. Spend your days basking in the sunshine on the town's sandy beaches, where you can swim, sunbathe, or partake in water sports such as sailing, windsurfing, and kayaking. Alternatively, lace up your hiking boots and explore the scenic trails that wind through olive groves, vineyards, and picturesque hillside villages, offering panoramic views of Lake Garda and the surrounding mountains.

Festivals and Events in Bardolino

Throughout the year, Bardolino comes alive with vibrant festivals and events that celebrate its rich cultural heritage and local traditions. From the lively Carnevale di Bardolino in February, featuring colorful parades and masquerade balls, to the festive Festa dell'Uva e del Vino Bardolino in September, where the town's streets are transformed into a bustling marketplace of wine, food, and entertainment, there's always something exciting happening in Bardolino. Be sure to check the event calendar and plan your visit accordingly to experience the magic of these unique celebrations.

Day Trips from Bardolino

While Bardolino offers more than enough attractions to keep visitors entertained, it also serves as an ideal base for exploring the surrounding area. Embark on a scenic boat cruise across Lake Garda to visit neighboring towns such as Lazise, Sirmione, and Malcesine, each offering its own distinct charm and attractions. Alternatively, venture inland to discover the historic cities of Ver

- Lazise

As I stood on the shores of Lake Garda, gazing out at the crystal-clear waters and the picturesque surroundings, I knew I had stumbled upon something truly special. Welcome to Lazise, a charming town nestled on the eastern shore of Lake Garda, where history, beauty, and tranquility converge to create an unforgettable destination.

Getting There

My journey to Lazise began with a scenic drive from Verona, winding through rolling hills and olive groves until I reached the shores of Lake Garda. For those arriving by air, Verona Airport is the closest international airport, just a short drive away from Lazise. Alternatively, you can also reach Lazise by train or bus, with regular services connecting Verona and other nearby cities to the town.

Where to Stay

Upon reaching Lazise, I was delighted to discover a variety of accommodation options catering to every budget and preference. Whether you're seeking luxury resorts, cozy bed and breakfasts, or family-friendly hotels, Lazise has it all. One of the highlights of my stay was the charming boutique hotels nestled within the historic town center, offering authentic Italian hospitality and stunning views of Lake Garda.

Exploring the Town

Stepping into the heart of Lazise, I found myself transported back in time, as narrow cobblestone streets lined with medieval buildings greeted me at every turn. The town's focal point is undoubtedly its picturesque harbor, where fishing boats bob gently in the water and waterfront cafes beckon visitors to relax and soak in the atmosphere.

One of the highlights of my time in Lazise was exploring the town's impressive medieval walls, which encircle the historic center and offer panoramic views of the surrounding landscape. As I wandered along the ramparts, I couldn't help but marvel at the centuries of history that permeate every stone.

Cuisine and Dining

No visit to Lazise would be complete without indulging in the region's world-renowned cuisine. From fresh seafood plucked straight from Lake Garda to hearty pasta dishes and decadent gelato, the town's restaurants offer a tantalizing array of flavors to suit every palate.

One of my most memorable dining experiences was enjoying a leisurely meal al fresco at one of the waterfront trattorias, where I savored delicious local specialties while watching the sun set over the lake. For those looking to immerse themselves in the culinary delights of the region, be sure to sample the famous olive oil produced in the surrounding countryside, as well as the region's renowned wines, such as Bardolino and Lugana.

Activities and Attractions

In addition to its natural beauty and historic charm, Lazise offers a wealth of activities and attractions to suit every interest. Outdoor enthusiasts will delight in the myriad of water sports available on Lake Garda, from sailing and windsurfing to kayaking and paddleboarding.

For those seeking a more leisurely pace, a leisurely stroll along the lakefront promenade is the perfect way to soak in the stunning scenery and vibrant atmosphere of Lazise. The town is also home to several cultural attractions, including the impressive Scaliger Castle, which dates back to the 9th century and offers fascinating insights into the region's medieval history.

Day Trips and Excursions

While Lazise itself is a treasure trove of attractions, its central location on Lake Garda makes it the perfect base for exploring the surrounding area. Nearby towns such as Bardolino, Sirmione, and Garda are just a short drive away and offer their own unique charms and attractions.

One of the highlights of my time in Lazise was taking a boat tour of Lake Garda, which allowed me to discover hidden coves, charming villages, and breathtaking vistas that can only be experienced from the water. Whether you're seeking adventure, relaxation, or cultural enrichment, Lazise and its surroundings offer endless possibilities for exploration and discovery.

- Malcesine

As I close my eyes, memories of Malcesine come flooding back – the gentle sway of the boats on Lake Garda, the scent of freshly baked pastries wafting through the air, and the sight of medieval architecture set against the backdrop of majestic mountains. Join me on a journey through this enchanting town on the shores of Italy's largest lake, as I guide you through its history, attractions, culinary delights, and hidden gems.

Introduction to Malcesine

Nestled on the eastern shore of Lake Garda, Malcesine is a picturesque town that embodies the essence of Italian charm. Its narrow cobblestone streets, colorful buildings, and medieval castle create a captivating ambiance that has enchanted visitors for centuries. As you wander through the town, you'll encounter a blend of history, culture, and natural beauty that is truly unparalleled.

Getting to Malcesine

Before diving into the heart of Malcesine, let's discuss how to get here. The nearest airport is Verona Airport, located approximately 60 kilometers away. From there, you can rent a car or take a bus to Malcesine. Alternatively, you can arrive by train to Peschiera del Garda or Desenzano del Garda and then take a ferry across the lake.

Exploring Malcesine

Scaliger Castle
One of Malcesine's most iconic landmarks is Scaliger Castle, a medieval fortress perched atop a rocky promontory overlooking the lake. Built in the 13th century by the Scaligeri family, the castle offers panoramic views of Lake Garda and the surrounding mountains. Inside, you'll find a museum showcasing historical artifacts and exhibits on the castle's rich history.

Monte Baldo Cable Car
For a bird's eye view of Lake Garda and the surrounding countryside, hop on the Monte Baldo Cable Car. This exhilarating ride takes you to the summit of Monte Baldo, where you can enjoy breathtaking vistas and explore hiking trails. Whether you're an adventure enthusiast or a nature lover, the cable car ride is a must-do experience in Malcesine.

Historic Center
Stroll through Malcesine's historic center and soak in the ambiance of its charming streets and squares. Admire the colorful facades of centuries-old buildings, browse quaint shops selling local crafts and souvenirs, and stop for a leisurely meal at one of the town's trattorias or cafes. Don't forget to

sample regional specialties like risotto al tartufo (truffle risotto) and gelato made with fresh, local ingredients.

Waterfront Promenade
No visit to Malcesine would be complete without a leisurely stroll along the waterfront promenade. Lined with palm trees and dotted with cafes and gelaterias, the promenade offers stunning views of the lake and the surrounding mountains. Take a seat on a bench, savor a gelato, and watch as boats sail lazily across the shimmering waters.

Day Trips from Malcesine

While Malcesine itself offers plenty to see and do, it also serves as a perfect base for exploring the surrounding area. Here are a few day trip ideas:

Sirmione
Located at the southern tip of Lake Garda, Sirmione is renowned for its thermal baths, ancient Roman ruins, and picturesque old town. Explore the ruins of the Grotte di Catullo, soak in the healing waters of the Terme di Sirmione, and wander through the narrow streets lined with shops and cafes.

Verona
Immerse yourself in the romantic atmosphere of Verona, the city of Romeo and Juliet. Visit Juliet's House, marvel at the ancient Roman amphitheater, and wander through the charming streets of the

historic center. Don't miss the chance to enjoy a traditional Veronese meal at a local osteria.

Garda Theme Parks
If you're traveling with kids (or just young at heart), consider a day trip to one of the theme parks near Lake Garda. Gardaland, Italy's largest amusement park, offers thrilling rides, shows, and attractions for visitors of all ages. Meanwhile, CanevaWorld Resort features water parks, a movie studio, and a medieval-themed area.

- Riva del Garda

Welcome to Riva del Garda, nestled on the picturesque shores of Lake Garda in northern Italy. As someone who has had the pleasure of exploring this charming town, I'm excited to share with you the wonders it has to offer. From breathtaking landscapes to rich history and vibrant culture, Riva del Garda is a destination that captivates the soul. Join me on a journey through this enchanting town as we uncover its hidden gems and cherished attractions.

Arriving in Riva del Garda

My journey to Riva del Garda began with a scenic drive through the rolling hills and vineyards of northern Italy. As I approached the shores of Lake Garda, the stunning vistas of crystal-clear waters and towering mountains greeted me, setting the stage for an unforgettable adventure. Whether you're arriving by car, bus, or ferry, the journey to Riva del Garda is sure to be filled with awe-inspiring views at every turn.

Accommodation Options

Upon arrival in Riva del Garda, I was spoilt for choice when it came to accommodation options. From charming boutique hotels to luxurious lakeside resorts, there's something to suit every taste and budget. During my stay, I opted for a cozy lakeside villa, offering panoramic views of Lake Garda and easy access to the town's attractions. However, if you prefer a more budget-friendly option, there are plenty of quaint guesthouses and bed-and-breakfasts nestled within Riva del Garda's historic streets.

Exploring the Town

Once settled into my accommodation, I set out to explore the charming streets of Riva del Garda. The town's historic center is a labyrinth of cobblestone alleyways, lined with colorful buildings adorned with cascading flowers. Wandering through the streets, I couldn't help but feel transported back in time, as I admired the well-preserved architecture and quaint cafes that dotted every corner.

Must-See Attractions

Riva del Garda is home to a wealth of must-see attractions, each offering a glimpse into the town's rich history and culture. One of the highlights of my visit was exploring the imposing Scaliger Castle, which overlooks the town from its perch atop a rocky outcrop. Built in the 13th century, this medieval fortress offers panoramic views of Lake Garda and houses a fascinating museum showcasing the town's maritime heritage.

For nature enthusiasts, a visit to the Varone Waterfall is a must. Located just a short drive from Riva del Garda, this spectacular waterfall cascades down a series of limestone cliffs, creating a mesmerizing display of natural beauty. A network of trails and viewing platforms allows visitors to explore the surrounding parkland and witness the power of the waterfall up close.

Outdoor Activities

As an outdoor enthusiast, I was thrilled to discover the myriad of outdoor activities available in Riva del Garda. From hiking and mountain biking to windsurfing and sailing, there's no shortage of adventures to be had on Lake Garda's pristine waters and rugged terrain. One of the highlights of my trip was embarking on a guided hike through the nearby Monte Brione Nature Reserve, where I was rewarded with sweeping views of the lake and surrounding mountains.

For those seeking adrenaline-fueled thrills, Riva del Garda is also a paradise for water sports enthusiasts. The town's favorable winds and crystal-clear waters make it the perfect destination for windsurfing, kiteboarding, and sailing. Whether you're a seasoned pro or a novice looking to try something new, there are plenty of rental shops and schools offering equipment and lessons to suit all skill levels.

Culinary Delights

No visit to Riva del Garda would be complete without indulging in the region's culinary delights. From fresh seafood caught daily from the lake to hearty mountain fare, the town's restaurants offer a diverse array of dishes to tantalize the taste buds. During my stay, I sampled traditional dishes such as risotto al pesce (fish risotto) and carne salada (cured beef), washed down with a glass of locally-produced wine from the nearby vineyards.

For a true taste of Italian gelato, a visit to one of Riva del Garda's gelaterias is a must. I couldn't resist indulging in a scoop (or two) of creamy gelato in flavors ranging from classic pistachio to exotic fruit combinations. Whether enjoyed as a midday treat or a sweet ending to a delicious meal, gelato is the perfect way to beat the heat and savor the flavors of Italy.

Shopping and Souvenirs

Before bidding farewell to Riva del Garda, be sure to explore the town's vibrant shopping scene. From boutique fashion stores to artisanal craft shops, there's something for everyone to discover. I spent hours wandering through the bustling market stalls, browsing handcrafted jewelry, leather goods, and locally-produced olive oil. Whether you're searching for the perfect souvenir or simply enjoying window shopping, Riva del Garda offers a treasure trove of unique finds waiting to be discovered.

CHAPTER FOUR

Activities at Lake Garda

- Water Sports: Sailing, Windsurfing, Kitesurfing

As I set foot in the breathtaking region surrounding Lake Garda, I couldn't help but feel exhilarated at the thought of the water sports adventures awaiting me. With its crystal-clear waters, stunning mountain backdrop, and consistent wind patterns, Lake Garda is a haven for sailing, windsurfing, and kitesurfing enthusiasts like myself.

Sailing:

Embarking on a sailing excursion across Lake Garda is an experience like no other. The gentle breeze caresses the sails as my vessel glides effortlessly across the water, offering panoramic views of the surrounding landscape. Whether you're a seasoned sailor or a novice, there are plenty of options available for exploring the lake by boat. From private charters to group tours, the possibilities are endless.

One of the highlights of sailing on Lake Garda is the opportunity to visit charming lakeside towns and villages along the way. From the historic streets of Sirmione to the picturesque harbor of Malcesine, each stop offers a glimpse into the rich culture and heritage of the region.

Windsurfing:

As I geared up for a windsurfing session on Lake Garda, I could feel the adrenaline coursing through my veins. With its consistent thermal winds and wide-open spaces, the lake provides the perfect playground for windsurfers of all skill levels. Whether you're gliding across the water with ease or mastering new tricks and techniques, there's no shortage of excitement to be found.

One of the best spots for windsurfing on Lake Garda is the northern town of Torbole. Here, the strong afternoon winds create ideal conditions for adrenaline-fueled rides and high-speed thrills. As I navigated the choppy waters and ride the waves, I couldn't help but marvel at the sheer beauty and power of nature surrounding me.

Kitesurfing:

For those seeking an even greater adrenaline rush, kitesurfing offers an unparalleled sense of freedom and excitement. With its combination of wind power and board control, kitesurfing allows me to soar through the air and perform awe-inspiring tricks with ease. Whether I'm launching off waves or catching air in flat water, the thrill of kitesurfing on Lake Garda is truly unmatched.

One of the best spots for kitesurfing on Lake Garda is the southern town of Malcesine. Here, the steady afternoon winds and spacious beaches provide the perfect conditions for riding the waves and catching big air. As I harnessed the power of the wind and carve through the water, I couldn't help but feel a sense of pure exhilaration coursing through my veins.

- Hiking and Trekking Trails

Essential Hiking and Trekking Tips

Before setting out on any hiking or trekking adventure, it's essential to be well-prepared. In this chapter, I'll share some valuable tips to ensure a safe and enjoyable experience on the trails of Lake Garda. From packing the right gear to staying hydrated and respecting the environment, these tips will help you make the most of your outdoor escapades.

Exploring Riva del Garda and Surroundings

Our journey begins in Riva del Garda, a charming town located at the northern tip of Lake Garda. From here, we'll discover an array of hiking trails that offer breathtaking views of the lake and surrounding mountains. Whether you're a beginner or an experienced trekker, Riva del Garda has something to offer for everyone.

Trekking Adventures in Malcesine and Monte Baldo

Next, we'll venture to Malcesine, a picturesque town famous for its medieval castle and cable car that ascends to Monte Baldo. Known as the "Garden of Europe," Monte Baldo boasts a network of scenic hiking trails that traverse lush meadows, rocky ridges, and alpine forests. Get ready to experience awe-inspiring panoramas of Lake Garda and the surrounding countryside.

Discovering Limone sul Garda and its Trails

Our exploration continues in Limone sul Garda, a quaint town nestled on the western shores of Lake Garda. Renowned for its lemon groves and Mediterranean climate, Limone sul Garda is a paradise for hikers and nature lovers. Join me as we hike through olive groves, vineyards, and ancient footpaths that reveal the rich history and natural beauty of this enchanting region.

Hidden Gems and Off-the-Beaten-Path Trails

In this chapter, I'll uncover some hidden gems and lesser-known trails that offer a more secluded and authentic hiking experience. From secret coves to hidden waterfalls, Lake Garda is full of surprises waiting to be discovered. Whether you're seeking solitude or adventure, these off-the-beaten-path trails will take you off the tourist track and into the heart of nature.

- Cycling Routes

As a fervent cyclist and avid traveler, the allure of Lake Garda's pristine shores and picturesque vistas has always captivated my imagination. Nestled amidst the majestic backdrop of the Italian Alps, this sprawling expanse of crystalline waters embodies an idyllic haven for outdoor enthusiasts and nature lovers alike.

Setting the Scene
Before delving into the intricacies of Lake Garda's cycling routes, it is imperative to paint a vivid portrait of this mesmerizing destination. Encompassing a surface area of approximately 143 square miles, Lake Garda stands as the largest lake in Italy, adorned with a myriad of charming towns and villages that exude timeless allure. From the

medieval charm of Sirmione to the bustling streets of Riva del Garda, each enclave along the lake's perimeter offers a unique blend of history, culture, and gastronomy waiting to be discovered.

The Cycling Culture
At the heart of Lake Garda's allure lies its vibrant cycling culture, which serves as a testament to the region's commitment to eco-friendly tourism and outdoor recreation. Whether you're a seasoned cyclist seeking adrenaline-pumping mountain trails or a leisurely pedaler in pursuit of scenic vistas, Lake Garda boasts an extensive network of cycling paths catering to enthusiasts of all skill levels. From family-friendly promenades to challenging mountain ascents, there's a cycling route tailor-made to suit every preference and ability.

Exploring the Cycling Routes
Armed with a sense of wanderlust and an insatiable thirst for adventure, I embarked on my cycling escapade, eager to traverse the diverse terrain that defines Lake Garda's cycling routes. From the tranquil shores of Lazise to the rugged terrain of Monte Baldo, each route offers a kaleidoscopic tapestry of sensory delights waiting to be experienced.

1. The Lakeside Promenade:
   Distance: Approximately 40 kilometers round-trip

Description: Meandering along the serene shores of Lake Garda, the Lakeside Promenade epitomizes the epitome of leisurely cycling, offering breathtaking views of the azure waters and verdant landscapes that define the region. Beginning in the charming town of Peschiera del Garda, this scenic route winds its way through quaint villages and picturesque vineyards, inviting cyclists to indulge in moments of tranquility amidst nature's embrace.

2. The Panoramic Loop:

Distance: Approximately 60 kilometers round-trip

Description For those seeking a more exhilarating cycling experience, the Panoramic Loop presents an enticing blend of challenging ascents and awe-inspiring vistas. Beginning in the bustling town of Malcesine, this route ascends towards the majestic heights of Monte Baldo, where cyclists are rewarded with panoramic views of the entire Lake Garda basin. As I navigate the winding mountain roads and steep gradients, a sense of exhilaration courses through my veins, fueled by the sheer majesty of the surrounding landscape.

3. The Valpolicella Wine Route:

Distance: Approximately 50 kilometers round-trip

Description: Indulging my passion for both cycling and oenology, the Valpolicella Wine Route emerges as a tantalizing fusion of gastronomic delights and scenic cycling. Beginning in the historic town of Bardolino, this route meanders through the sun-drenched vineyards and rolling hills of the Valpolicella wine region, where the tantalizing aromas of Amarone and Ripasso beckon weary travelers to pause and savor the fruits of the land.

4. The Dolomite Challenge:

Distance: Approximately 100 kilometers round-trip

Description:For intrepid cyclists seeking the ultimate test of endurance and skill, the Dolomite Challenge offers an unparalleled opportunity to conquer the majestic peaks and rugged terrain of the Italian Alps. Beginning in the quaint village of Arco, this route traverses the awe-inspiring landscapes of the Dolomites, where winding mountain roads and steep inclines beckon cyclists to push beyond their limits and embrace the thrill of adventure.

Tips for Cyclists

As I reflected on my cycling escapades along the shores of Lake Garda, I was compelled to share a few invaluable tips for fellow enthusiasts embarking on their own journey of exploration:

1. Gear Up: Ensure that your bicycle is well-maintained and equipped with essential gear such as helmets, water bottles, and repair kits to ensure a safe and enjoyable ride.
2. Stay Hydrated: With the sun-drenched landscapes of Lake Garda as your backdrop, it's

essential to stay hydrated throughout your cycling adventures. Carry an ample supply of water and replenish your fluids regularly to avoid dehydration.

3. Respect Nature: As custodians of the environment, it is our responsibility to tread lightly and minimize our ecological footprint while cycling along Lake Garda's pristine shores. Respect wildlife, adhere to designated trails, and dispose of waste responsibly to preserve the region's natural beauty for future generations to enjoy.

4. Embrace the Journey: Whether you're navigating the tranquil lakeside promenades or conquering the rugged peaks of the Dolomites, remember to savor every moment of your cycling journey along Lake Garda. Embrace the sense of freedom, exhilaration, and camaraderie that accompanies life on two wheels, and let the rhythm of your pedal strokes guide you towards new horizons of discovery.

- Golfing

As a passionate golfer, exploring the verdant landscapes surrounding Lake Garda was a dream come true. While the azure waters of Italy's largest lake offer endless opportunities for relaxation and water activities, the lush countryside hides a golfer's paradise waiting to be discovered.

Introduction to Golfing Near Lake Garda

Nestled amidst the rolling hills and picturesque vineyards of northern Italy, Lake Garda is renowned for its stunning natural beauty and Mediterranean climate. While golf may not be the first thing that comes to mind when envisioning this idyllic destination, the region boasts several world-class golf courses that cater to players of all skill levels.

Golf Courses Near Lake Garda

1. Garda Golf Country Club: Located just a short drive from the shores of Lake Garda, Garda Golf Country Club offers a challenging 27-hole course set against the backdrop of the Alps. Designed by British architects Cotton, Pennink & Partners, this championship course features immaculately manicured fairways, pristine greens, and breathtaking views of the surrounding countryside.

2. Golf Club Paradiso del Garda: Situated on the eastern shores of Lake Garda, Golf Club Paradiso del Garda is a golfer's oasis surrounded by lush olive groves and vineyards. This 18-hole course, designed by renowned architect Jim Fazio, seamlessly blends natural beauty with strategic challenges, making it a must-play for golf enthusiasts visiting the region.

3. Chervò Golf San Vigilio: Perched atop the picturesque hills overlooking Lake Garda, Chervò Golf San Vigilio offers three distinct nine-hole courses that wind their way through centuries-old olive trees, sparkling lakes, and ancient ruins. With its unique layout and stunning vistas, this award-winning golf resort provides an unforgettable golfing experience for players of all abilities.

4. Arzaga Golf Club: Located just a short drive from Lake Garda, Arzaga Golf Club boasts two championship courses designed by golfing legends Jack Nicklaus and Gary Player. Set amidst the rolling hills of the Valtenesi region, these meticulously landscaped courses offer a perfect blend of challenge and natural beauty, making them a favorite among golfers from around the world.

Planning Your Golfing Adventure

Before embarking on your golfing adventure near Lake Garda, it's essential to plan ahead to ensure a memorable experience. Here are some tips to help you make the most of your time on the links:

1. Book Tee Times in Advance: Many of the top golf courses near Lake Garda can get busy, especially during peak season. Be sure to book your tee times well in advance to secure your preferred playing times and avoid disappointment.

2. Pack Accordingly: When packing for your golfing excursion, be sure to bring along all the necessary equipment, including clubs, balls, tees, and appropriate attire. Additionally, don't forget to pack sunscreen, sunglasses, and a hat to protect yourself from the sun's rays.

3. Explore Off-Course Activities: While golf may be the main focus of your trip, be sure to take some time to explore the other attractions and activities that Lake Garda has to offer. From scenic boat cruises and watersports to wine tasting and cultural excursions, there's something for everyone to enjoy in this enchanting region.

4. Immerse Yourself in the Local Cuisine: No trip to Italy would be complete without indulging in the country's world-renowned cuisine. Be sure to sample the delicious local dishes and wines at the golf club restaurants and nearby trattorias for an authentic taste of Italian gastronomy.

- Spa and Wellness Centers

As a traveler exploring the stunning region of Lake Garda, I couldn't help but be captivated by its natural beauty, charming villages, and rich history.

Amidst the picturesque landscapes and cultural treasures, one aspect that stands out for relaxation and rejuvenation is the plethora of spa and wellness centers dotted around the lake.

Understanding Spa and Wellness in Lake Garda:

Before delving into specific spa and wellness centers, it's essential to understand the significance of this aspect in Lake Garda's tourism industry. The region's natural geothermal springs have long been revered for their therapeutic properties, making Lake Garda a haven for spa enthusiasts. Whether you're seeking traditional spa treatments, holistic healing therapies, or simply want to unwind in a serene environment, Lake Garda offers a wide range of options to cater to your wellness needs.

Exploring Spa and Wellness Centers:

1. Aquaria Thermal Spa & Wellness Center (Sirmione): Situated on the shores of Lake Garda in the historic town of Sirmione, Aquaria Thermal Spa offers a holistic approach to wellness amidst breathtaking surroundings. The spa's thermal waters, rich in minerals and trace elements, are believed to have healing properties beneficial for various ailments. From thermal baths and hydrotherapy to massages and beauty treatments, Aquaria provides a comprehensive wellness experience that rejuvenates both body and mind. As I stepped into the tranquil ambiance of Aquaria, I

was greeted by the soothing sound of cascading water and the calming aroma of essential oils, instantly transporting me into a state of relaxation.

2. Garda Thermae (Arco): Located in the picturesque town of Arco, Garda Thermae is a modern wellness center that embraces the natural elements of the surrounding landscape. Set against the backdrop of towering cliffs and lush greenery, Garda Thermae offers a range of wellness programs tailored to individual needs. Whether you're indulging in a therapeutic massage overlooking the panoramic views of Lake Garda or participating in a yoga session amidst nature, Garda Thermae provides a serene sanctuary for holistic healing. During my visit to Garda Thermae, I was impressed by the seamless integration of contemporary spa facilities with the tranquil beauty of the outdoors, creating a harmonious retreat for wellness seekers.

3. Villa dei Cedri Thermal Park & Hotel (Lazise):Tucked away in the charming town of Lazise, Villa dei Cedri Thermal Park & Hotel is a hidden gem renowned for its expansive thermal park and luxurious spa facilities. The centerpiece of the thermal park is the ancient thermal lake, fed by natural hot springs that emerge from deep underground. Guests can immerse themselves in the therapeutic waters of the thermal lake, surrounded by lush gardens and centuries-old cedars. In addition to the thermal lake, Villa dei Cedri offers a variety of spa treatments, including

massages, facials, and body wraps, all designed to promote relaxation and well-being. My experience at Villa dei Cedri was nothing short of magical, as I soaked in the healing waters of the thermal lake while being enveloped by the tranquility of the park.

4. Lefay Resort & SPA Lago di Garda (Gargnano): Perched on the hills overlooking Lake Garda, Lefay Resort & SPA Lago di Garda is a luxurious wellness retreat that combines modern amenities with eco-friendly practices. The resort's holistic approach to wellness is reflected in its state-of-the-art spa facilities, which include indoor and outdoor pools, saunas, steam rooms, and a wide range of therapeutic treatments. From traditional Chinese medicine and Ayurveda to Western spa therapies, Lefay offers a comprehensive menu of wellness programs tailored to individual needs. During my stay at Lefay, I was impressed by the serene ambiance of the resort, as well as the impeccable service and attention to detail that enhanced my wellness experience.

5. Hotel Caesius Thermae & SPA Resort (Bardolino): Situated in the charming town of Bardolino, Hotel Caesius Thermae & SPA Resort is a haven of tranquility and relaxation overlooking Lake Garda. The resort's extensive spa facilities include thermal pools, saunas, Turkish baths, and a wide range of wellness treatments inspired by ancient Roman traditions. Guests can indulge in

therapeutic massages, facials, and body rituals using natural ingredients sourced from the region. As I immersed myself in the soothing waters of the thermal pools at Hotel Caesius, I couldn't help but feel a sense of serenity wash over me, providing a much-needed escape from the hustle and bustle of everyday life.

CHAPTER FIVE

Cultural and Historical Attractions

- Scaliger Castle in Sirmione

Welcome to Lake Garda, a gem nestled in the heart of Northern Italy, where history, culture, and natural beauty intertwine seamlessly. As you embark on your adventure around this enchanting lake, one landmark stands out amidst the picturesque scenery - Scaliger Castle in Sirmione.

Join me as we delve into the rich history and captivating allure of this medieval fortress.

The Origins of Scaliger Castle

As we approach the peninsula of Sirmione, the silhouette of Scaliger Castle emerges, commanding attention with its formidable presence. The castle, also known as Castello Scaligero, dates back to the 13th century and is steeped in history. It was commissioned by the Scaliger family, powerful rulers of Verona, who sought to establish their dominance over the region.

Unraveling the Architectural Marvels

Stepping through the ancient gates of Scaliger Castle is akin to stepping back in time. The castle is a masterpiece of medieval architecture, characterized by its robust stone walls, crenellated towers, and a moat that once served as a defensive barrier. As we wandered through the inner courtyard, we are greeted by the sight of well-preserved battlements and majestic ramparts, offering panoramic views of Lake Garda and the surrounding landscape.

A Glimpse into Medieval Life

Within the confines of Scaliger Castle, visitors have the opportunity to explore a labyrinth of chambers and corridors that once bustled with activity. From the grand halls adorned with frescoes to the intimate living quarters of the ruling family, each room offers a glimpse into the daily life of medieval aristocracy. As we admire the intricate craftsmanship of the furnishings and artifacts on display, we can't help but marvel at the ingenuity and artistry of the era.

Legends and Lore of Scaliger Castle

No visit to Scaliger Castle would be complete without delving into the legends and lore that shroud its storied past. Tales of noble knights, star-crossed lovers, and daring sieges abound, adding an air of mystery and intrigue to the castle's ambiance. One of the most enduring legends is that of the ghost of Queen Adelaide, whose spirit is said to wander the castle grounds in search of her lost love.

Scaliger Castle Today: Preservation and Conservation

In recent years, efforts have been made to preserve and restore Scaliger Castle, ensuring that future generations can continue to appreciate its historical significance. Restoration projects have focused on reinforcing the structure, conserving precious artifacts, and enhancing visitor experiences through interactive exhibits and educational programs.

Today, Scaliger Castle stands as a testament to the enduring legacy of Italy's medieval heritage.

Exploring Sirmione Beyond Scaliger Castle

While Scaliger Castle undoubtedly takes center stage in Sirmione, there is much more to explore in this charming lakeside town. From the ancient ruins of the Grotte di Catullo to the bustling streets lined with quaint shops and cafes, Sirmione offers a treasure trove of delights waiting to be discovered. Be sure to indulge in the local cuisine, sample regional wines, and take leisurely strolls along the lakefront promenade for a truly immersive experience.

Practical Information for Visitors

Before you embark on your journey to Scaliger Castle, here are a few practical tips to ensure a smooth and enjoyable visit:

- Opening Hours: Scaliger Castle is open to visitors throughout the year, with varying hours depending on the season. Be sure to check the official website for up-to-date information on opening hours and guided tours.

- Admission Fees: There is a nominal fee for entry to Scaliger Castle, with discounts available for children, students, and seniors. Tickets can be purchased on-site or online in advance to avoid long queues during peak tourist season.

- Accessibility: While Scaliger Castle is a historic site with uneven terrain and narrow staircases, efforts have been made to improve accessibility for visitors with mobility issues. Wheelchair ramps and elevators are available in certain areas, but some sections may still be challenging to navigate.

- Guided Tours: To make the most of your visit to Scaliger Castle, consider joining a guided tour led by knowledgeable local guides. Guided tours provide valuable insights into the castle's history, architecture, and significance, enhancing the overall experience.

- Grotte di Catullo in Sirmione

Getting Acquainted with Grotte di Catullo:

Perched atop the Sirmione peninsula, at the southern tip of Lake Garda, lies the archaeological site of Grotte di Catullo. Named after the famous Roman poet Gaius Valerius Catullus, who was believed to have owned a villa on the site during the

1st century BCE, the Grotte di Catullo is steeped in history and mythology.

Unraveling the History:

As we step back in time, let's unravel the layers of history that shroud the Grotte di Catullo. Originally constructed during the Roman Republic, the villa underwent several phases of expansion and renovation under the ownership of various noble families. Its strategic location provided breathtaking views of the surrounding landscape while serving as a retreat for the elite of ancient Rome.

Exploring the Ruins:

Walking through the ruins of Grotte di Catullo, one can't help but marvel at the architectural grandeur of the past. Despite centuries of decay and plunder, the remains of the villa's thermal baths, courtyards, and terraces offer glimpses into the opulent lifestyle of its former inhabitants. From the imposing foundations of the main residence to the intricate mosaic floors that once adorned its halls, each stone tells a story of bygone splendor.

Myth and Legend:

Beyond its historical significance, Grotte di Catullo is shrouded in myth and legend. According to local folklore, the nearby Grotte di Catullo cave was believed to be the home of the Sirens, mythical creatures whose enchanting songs lured sailors to their doom. This mystical connection adds an aura of mystery to the site, inviting visitors to ponder the tales of the past as they wander its ancient ruins.

Natural Beauty Surrounding the Site:

As we explore the grounds of Grotte di Catullo, it's impossible to ignore the breathtaking beauty of its natural surroundings. Perched on the edge of Lake Garda, the villa offers panoramic views of the azure waters and distant mountains, creating a picturesque backdrop for our journey through time. Lush vegetation, including olive trees and cypress groves, adds to the idyllic setting, inviting visitors to pause and soak in the tranquility of the landscape.

Practical Information for Visitors:

For travelers planning a visit to Grotte di Catullo, it's essential to come prepared. The site is accessible via a scenic walk from the town of Sirmione, where visitors can explore charming cobblestone streets, historic landmarks, and local eateries. Comfortable walking shoes, sunscreen, and plenty of water are recommended, especially during the warm summer months when temperatures can soar.

Tips for a Memorable Experience:

To make the most of your visit to Grotte di Catullo, consider the following tips:

1. Timing: Arrive early in the day to avoid crowds and make the most of your time exploring the ruins.
2. Guided Tours: Consider joining a guided tour to gain insight into the history and significance of the site from knowledgeable experts.
3. Photography: Don't forget your camera! Grotte di Catullo offers numerous photo opportunities, from panoramic vistas to intricate architectural details.
4. Picnic: Pack a picnic lunch and enjoy a leisurely meal amidst the tranquil surroundings of the villa's terraces or nearby park.
5. Exploration: Take your time to wander through the ruins at your own pace, soaking in the atmosphere and imagining life in ancient Rome.

- Vittoriale degli Italiani in Gardone Riviera

As I stood on the shores of Lake Garda, I was overwhelmed by the sheer magnificence that surrounds me. With its crystal-clear waters reflecting the towering peaks of the Alps, Lake Garda is not just a destination; it's an experience.

And nestled along its shores are two gems of history and culture that are must-visits for any traveler: the Vittoriale degli Italiani and the Grotte di Catullo.

Vittoriale degli Italiani: A Monument to Genius and Eccentricity

My journey begins with a visit to the Vittoriale degli Italiani, a sprawling complex nestled in the hills overlooking Lake Garda. Built as a tribute to the poet and war hero Gabriele D'Annunzio, the Vittoriale is a fascinating blend of architectural styles, lush gardens, and quirky memorabilia that offers a glimpse into the mind of one of Italy's most enigmatic figures.

As I stepped through the ornate gates of the Vittoriale, I was immediately struck by the grandeur of the place. The main villa, known as the Prioria, is a masterpiece of eclectic design, with its terracotta walls, intricate mosaics, and sweeping views of the lake below. But it's not just the architecture that captivates me; it's the sheer eccentricity of the place. Everywhere I look, there are reminders of D'Annunzio's larger-than-life personality, from the vintage cars parked in the courtyard to the giant bronze prow of a battleship jutting out from the garden.

But amid the extravagance, there are also moments of quiet reflection. The mausoleum where D'Annunzio is buried is a solemn reminder of the sacrifices made during Italy's tumultuous history, while the amphitheater carved into the hillside offers a serene spot to take in a performance or simply soak up the atmosphere.

As I wandered through the labyrinthine corridors and hidden gardens of the Vittoriale, I couldn't help but feel a sense of awe at the sheer audacity of D'Annunzio's vision. Love him or loathe him, there's no denying the impact he had on Italian culture and politics, and the Vittoriale stands as a testament to his enduring legacy.

Grotte di Catullo: A Journey Back in Time

After immersing myself in the grandeur of the Vittoriale, I made my way to the Grotte di Catullo, a Roman archaeological site located on the tip of the Sirmione peninsula. Named after the Roman poet Catullus, who is said to have owned a villa nearby, the Grotte di Catullo is one of the most important historical sites in northern Italy, offering a fascinating glimpse into the lives of the ancient Romans who once called this area home.

As I approached the site, I was struck by the sheer scale of the ruins. Stretching over several acres, the Grotte di Catullo is an imposing sight, with its crumbling walls and weathered columns standing as silent witnesses to the passage of time. But despite the ravages of centuries, there's still an undeniable sense of grandeur to the place, with its panoramic views of the lake and surrounding countryside.

Wandering among the ruins, I couldn't help but marvel at the ingenuity of the ancient Romans who built this magnificent complex. From the intricate mosaic floors to the soaring arches of the main villa, every detail speaks to the skill and craftsmanship of those who came before us. And as I stood amidst the ruins, I can almost hear the echoes of laughter and conversation that once filled these hallowed halls.

But amidst the grandeur, there's also a sense of melancholy. The Grotte di Catullo is a reminder of the fragility of human civilization, and of the impermanence of our achievements. And yet, it's also a testament to the enduring spirit of resilience and renewal that has characterized this region for millennia.

- Rocca Scaligera in Malcesine

As I walked along the cobblestone streets of Malcesine, a picturesque town nestled on the eastern shore of Lake Garda, my eyes were drawn to the imposing silhouette of Rocca Scaligera rising proudly against the azure sky. This medieval fortress, steeped in history and surrounded by breathtaking natural beauty, is a testament to the rich heritage of this enchanting region.

Rocca Scaligera stands as a sentinel overlooking the town and the shimmering waters of Lake Garda, its massive stone walls and imposing towers evoking a sense of grandeur and strength. As I approached the fortress, I was struck by its commanding presence and the intricate details of its architecture, a perfect blend of medieval military prowess and artistic elegance.

Stepping through the ancient gates of Rocca Scaligera, I was transported back in time to an era of knights and noble lords, when castles stood as symbols of power and prestige. Inside the fortress, a labyrinth of winding corridors, hidden chambers, and soaring battlements awaits, inviting me to explore its secrets and uncover its storied past.

Climbing to the top of the tallest tower, I was rewarded with panoramic views of Malcesine and the surrounding landscape, the sparkling waters of Lake Garda stretching out before me like a vast azure expanse. From this vantage point, I could see the snow-capped peaks of the Alps in the distance, a striking contrast to the sun-drenched shores below.

Descending from the heights of Rocca Scaligera, I made my way to the shores of Lake Garda, where another marvel of ancient history awaits – the Grotte di Catullo. Nestled amidst lush greenery on the tip of the Sirmione peninsula, these ancient Roman ruins are a testament to the enduring legacy of one of history's greatest civilizations.

As I wandered through the ruins of the Grotte di Catullo, I was struck by the sheer scale and grandeur of this archaeological site. The remains of a vast Roman villa, once the luxurious retreat of a wealthy patrician family, lie scattered across the landscape, their weathered stone walls whispering tales of a bygone era.

Exploring the ruins, I was transported back in time to the height of the Roman Empire, imagining the opulent feasts and lavish celebrations that once took place within these hallowed halls. From the terraces overlooking the lake, I could almost hear the laughter of ancient revelers and the echoes of their footsteps as they danced beneath the stars.

As the sun begins to set over Lake Garda, casting a golden glow upon the ancient ruins, I found myself filled with a sense of awe and wonder at the timeless beauty of this place. In the fading light, the Grotte di Catullo takes on an ethereal quality, its ancient stones bathed in the soft hues of twilight.

As I reluctantly tore myself away from this enchanting scene, I know that I will carry the memories of Rocca Scaligera and the Grotte di Catullo with me forever. These timeless treasures of Lake Garda have left an indelible mark on my soul, reminding me of the enduring power of history and the timeless allure of Italy's most enchanting lake.

- Roman Ruins in Desenzano del Garda

As I stepped onto the sun-drenched streets of Desenzano del Garda, the vibrant atmosphere and rich history immediately captivated my senses. Located on the southwestern shore of the breathtaking Lake Garda, Desenzano del Garda is not only renowned for its stunning landscapes but also for its fascinating Roman ruins that offer a glimpse into the region's ancient past. Join me on a journey through time as we uncover the secrets of the Roman ruins in Desenzano del Garda, immersing ourselves in history, culture, and the unparalleled beauty of Lake Garda.

As I strolled through the town's bustling piazzas and labyrinthine alleyways, I couldn't help but marvel at the seamless blend of ancient history and modernity that defines Desenzano del Garda. From its well-preserved Roman ruins to its vibrant cafe culture and lively waterfront promenade, every corner of this enchanting town tells a story waiting to be discovered.

Uncovering the Roman Ruins

One of the highlights of my visit to Desenzano del Garda was exploring the town's impressive Roman ruins, which serve as a tangible reminder of its ancient past. The most prominent archaeological site in Desenzano del Garda is the Villa Romana, a sprawling complex that once served as a luxurious residence for wealthy Roman families.

As I entered the Villa Romana, I was immediately struck by the grandeur of its ruins, which include well-preserved mosaics, frescoes, and architectural features that offer insight into the daily lives of its former inhabitants. Walking through the ancient corridors and courtyards, I could almost imagine the bustling activity that once filled these hallowed halls, from lavish banquets to scholarly debates.

One of the highlights of the Villa Romana is its magnificent mosaic floors, which are adorned with intricate patterns and vibrant colors that have stood the test of time. Each mosaic tells a story, depicting scenes from mythology, daily life, and the natural world with astonishing detail and artistry. As I marveled at these ancient works of art, I couldn't help but feel a sense of wonder at the skill and craftsmanship of the artisans who created them.

In addition to the Villa Romana, Desenzano del Garda is also home to other significant Roman ruins, including the Grottoes of Catullus, which are located on the picturesque Sirmione peninsula just a short distance from the town center. These ancient ruins, which overlook the shimmering waters of Lake Garda, are believed to have once been part of a grand Roman villa and offer panoramic views of the surrounding landscape.

Exploring Desenzano del Garda

Beyond its Roman ruins, Desenzano del Garda offers a wealth of attractions and activities for visitors to enjoy. The town's charming historic center is perfect for leisurely strolls, with its narrow streets lined with quaint shops, cafes, and gelaterias offering irresistible treats.

One of the highlights of my time in Desenzano del Garda was exploring its vibrant waterfront promenade, which stretches along the shores of Lake Garda and offers stunning views of the lake and surrounding mountains. Whether savoring a delicious gelato, soaking up the sun on the beach, or taking a leisurely boat ride on the lake, there's no shortage of ways to enjoy the natural beauty of Lake Garda from the town's waterfront.

For those interested in history and culture, Desenzano del Garda is home to several museums and cultural institutions that offer insights into the town's storied past. The Museum of Archaeology, located in the heart of the historic center, showcases artifacts from prehistoric times to the Middle Ages, providing a fascinating glimpse into the region's rich archaeological heritage.

Culinary Delights

No visit to Desenzano del Garda would be complete without indulging in the region's delicious culinary offerings. From fresh seafood caught in the waters of Lake Garda to hearty pasta dishes and flavorful local wines, the town's restaurants and trattorias are a feast for the senses.

During my stay in Desenzano del Garda, I had the pleasure of sampling some of the region's specialties, including risotto alla pescatora, a mouthwatering seafood risotto, and lugana, a crisp white wine produced in the surrounding vineyards. Whether dining al fresco overlooking the lake or cozying up in a traditional trattoria, the flavors of Lake Garda never failed to delight and inspire.

CHAPTER SIX

Culinary Delights of Lake Garda

- Traditional Dishes and Local Cuisine

Nestled in the picturesque landscape of northern Italy, Lake Garda boasts a diverse culinary heritage shaped by its history, geography, and cultural influences. From rustic trattorias to elegant lakeside restaurants, there's no shortage of dining options to tantalize your taste buds.

The Influence of Geography and Climate

Before delving into specific dishes, it's essential to understand how Lake Garda's geography and climate influence its culinary offerings. The lake's mild climate and fertile soil create ideal conditions for agriculture, allowing the region to produce a bounty of fresh fruits, vegetables, and herbs. Additionally, the lake's pristine waters are home to a variety of fish, including trout, carp, and pike, which play a significant role in local cuisine.

Exploring Traditional Dishes

1. Risotto al Pesce Persico: A signature dish of Lake Garda, risotto al pesce persico features tender fillets of local whitefish delicately cooked with creamy Arborio rice, onions, white wine, and a hint of saffron. The result is a luxurious risotto bursting with flavors of the lake.

2. Trota alla Griglia: Grilled trout is a beloved staple of Lake Garda's culinary repertoire. Freshly caught trout is seasoned with aromatic herbs, olive oil, and lemon before being grilled to perfection. The simplicity of this dish allows the natural flavors of the fish to shine through, making it a favorite among locals and visitors alike.

3. Polenta e Luganega: This hearty dish combines creamy polenta with Luganega sausage, a coiled pork sausage seasoned with garlic, fennel seeds, and white wine. The sausage is grilled or pan-fried until golden brown, then served alongside a generous portion of velvety polenta. It's comfort food at its finest, perfect for chilly evenings by the lake.

4. Sarde in Saor: Hailing from the nearby region of Veneto, Sarde in Saor is a traditional dish featuring marinated sardines. The fish are gently fried until crispy, then layered with sweet and sour onions, vinegar, pine nuts, and raisins. The resulting flavor

combination is complex and addictive, showcasing the region's culinary heritage.

Regional Variations and Specialty Ingredients

While these dishes represent some of the quintessential flavors of Lake Garda, it's essential to note that each town and village around the lake may have its own unique specialties and variations. Whether it's the creamy gelato of Sirmione, the fragrant olive oil of Bardolino, or the artisanal cheeses of Limone sul Garda, exploring the diverse culinary landscape of Lake Garda is a journey of discovery.

Exploring Local Markets and Food Festivals

No visit to Lake Garda would be complete without immersing yourself in its vibrant food culture by visiting local markets and food festivals. From the bustling market in Desenzano del Garda, where you can sample freshly harvested produce and artisanal cheeses, to the annual Sagra del Pesce in Garda, a celebration of all things fish-related, these culinary experiences offer insight into the region's gastronomic traditions.

- Wine Tasting Tours

As a Lake Garda travel guide, let me immerse you in the delightful world of wine tasting tours around this stunning region. Nestled in the picturesque landscape of northern Italy, Lake Garda offers a plethora of vineyards and wineries waiting to be explored.

Embark on a journey through the vine-covered hills surrounding Lake Garda, where centuries-old traditions meet modern winemaking techniques. Begin your adventure with a visit to one of the renowned wineries in the area, such as Cantina Zeni or Ca' dei Frati, where you'll have the opportunity to sample a diverse range of wines, from crisp whites to robust reds.

As you sip and savor each glass, let the flavors transport you to the sun-drenched slopes where the grapes were lovingly cultivated. Learn about the unique terroir of the region, influenced by the lake's microclimate and the surrounding mountains, which impart distinct characteristics to the wines produced here.

No wine tasting tour would be complete without indulging in the local cuisine, and Lake Garda offers an abundance of culinary delights to pair with your favorite wines. From fresh seafood caught in the lake to hearty pasta dishes and creamy risottos, there's something to please every palate.

After a leisurely lunch overlooking the glistening waters of Lake Garda, continue your wine tasting adventure with a visit to a family-owned vineyard, where you'll have the chance to meet the winemakers themselves and gain insight into their craft. Stroll through the vineyards, breathe in the fragrant aromas of ripening grapes, and feel the connection to the land that produces such exquisite wines.

As the day draws to a close, take a moment to reflect on the beauty and bounty of Lake Garda, where the art of winemaking is woven into the fabric of daily life. Whether you're a seasoned oenophile or simply looking to discover something new, a wine tasting tour in Lake Garda promises an unforgettable experience that will tantalize your senses and leave you longing to return again and again.

- Olive Oil Tasting

My adventure began at a quaint olive grove nestled along the shores of Lake Garda. The air was filled with the subtle scent of olives, mingling with the fragrant aroma of Mediterranean herbs. Surrounded by the lush greenery of the grove, I felt a sense of tranquility wash over me as I eagerly awaited my olive oil tasting experience.

As I stepped into the rustic farmhouse, I was greeted by the warm smiles of the local artisans who had dedicated their lives to the art of olive oil production. They welcomed me with open arms, eager to share their knowledge and passion for this ancient tradition.

The tasting room was adorned with wooden barrels and terracotta jars, each containing a unique variety of olive oil. The soft glow of sunlight filtered through the windows, casting a golden hue over the room and illuminating the rich colors of the oils.

I was handed a delicate glass and invited to take a seat at a long wooden table adorned with freshly baked bread, ripe tomatoes, and fragrant herbs. The stage was set for a sensory journey unlike any other.

As I dipped a piece of crusty bread into the first sample of olive oil, my taste buds were instantly awakened by the vibrant flavors dancing on my palate. The oil was smooth and velvety, with notes of fresh grass and a hint of peppery spice. It was a revelation, a testament to the skill and expertise of the artisans who had crafted it.

With each subsequent tasting, I was transported on a culinary voyage through the diverse terroirs of Lake Garda. From the delicate sweetness of oils pressed from early-harvested green olives to the robust intensity of oils made from fully ripened fruit, each variety told a story of its own.

But it wasn't just the flavors that captivated me; it was the passion and dedication of the people behind the oil. As I listened to their stories, I gained a newfound appreciation for the centuries-old traditions that had been passed down through generations.

One particularly memorable moment was when I had the opportunity to witness the olive oil pressing process firsthand. The rhythmic hum of the ancient stone mill filled the air as ripe olives were slowly crushed into a fragrant paste. It was a labor of love, a delicate dance between tradition and innovation.

As the day drew to a close, I reflected on my olive oil tasting experience with a sense of gratitude and awe. Not only had I sampled some of the finest oils Lake Garda had to offer, but I had also gained a deeper understanding of the region's rich cultural heritage.

For me, Lake Garda would always be more than just a picturesque destination; it was a place where time stood still, where ancient traditions thrived, and where the simple act of tasting olive oil became a profound and unforgettable experience.

CHAPTER SEVEN

Shopping and Markets

- Local Markets

As I meandered through the charming towns surrounding Lake Garda, I couldn't help but be captivated by the bustling local markets that dot the picturesque landscape. These markets offer a vibrant tapestry of colors, scents, and sounds, each one a reflection of the rich culture and heritage of this enchanting region. Join me as I delve into the world of local markets in Lake Garda, exploring their unique offerings, traditions, and hidden treasures.

Exploring the Markets:
One of the highlights of any visit to Lake Garda is undoubtedly the opportunity to explore its vibrant markets, where locals and tourists alike converge to sample the region's finest produce, artisanal crafts, and culinary delights. From the bustling streets of Desenzano del Garda to the quaint squares of Bardolino, each market offers a unique experience, reflecting the distinct character of its host town.

Desenzano del Garda Market:

As I made my way through the narrow streets of Desenzano del Garda, I was immediately drawn to the lively atmosphere of its weekly market. Held every Tuesday morning, this bustling market is a treasure trove of local delights, from fresh fruits and vegetables to handmade leather goods and colorful ceramics. The air is filled with the aroma of freshly baked bread and roasted coffee, while vendors call out to passersby, tempting them with their wares. I weave my way through the crowds, sampling olives, cheeses, and cured meats, savoring the flavors of the region with each bite. The market is also a feast for the eyes, with stalls overflowing with vibrant flowers, delicate lacework, and intricately woven textiles. It's a true celebration of the local culture and a testament to the enduring charm of traditional markets in Lake Garda.

Bardolino Market:

Next, I found myself in the picturesque town of Bardolino, where the weekly market takes place every Thursday along the scenic waterfront promenade. The setting couldn't be more idyllic, with panoramic views of the lake providing a stunning backdrop to the bustling market below. Here, I was greeted by a kaleidoscope of colors as vendors display their goods beneath brightly colored umbrellas, their voices mingling with the sound of lapping waves and chirping seagulls. The market offers a delightful mix of local specialties, from fragrant olive oils and aromatic spices to handmade jewelry and intricately woven textiles. I was particularly drawn to the stalls selling fresh seafood, their displays piled high with glistening fish and shellfish caught that very morning. I indulged in a plate of freshly shucked oysters, savoring their briny sweetness as I soaked in the vibrant atmosphere of the market.

Riva del Garda Market:
No exploration of Lake Garda's markets would be complete without a visit to the charming town of Riva del Garda, home to one of the region's most renowned markets. Held every Saturday morning in the historic Piazza III Novembre, this bustling market is a kaleidoscope of sights, sounds, and scents that transport visitors back in time. Here, amidst the elegant Renaissance buildings and ancient cobblestone streets, I discovered a treasure trove of local delights, from artisanal cheeses and cured meats to handmade pottery and intricately carved wooden souvenirs. The market is a feast for the senses, with vendors proudly showcasing their goods and engaging in lively banter with customers. I was captivated by the skill and craftsmanship on display, marveling at the intricate designs of handmade lace and the rich hues of locally produced wines. As I wandered through the market, I was struck by the sense of community and camaraderie that permeates the air, a testament to the enduring appeal of traditional markets in Lake Garda.

Garda Market:
My journey through Lake Garda's markets culminates in the charming town of Garda, where the weekly market takes place every Friday morning along the picturesque lakeside promenade. Here, amidst the stunning backdrop of azure waters and verdant hills, I was greeted by a vibrant array of stalls selling everything from fresh produce and flowers to handmade crafts and souvenirs. The atmosphere is electric, with locals and tourists alike mingling amidst the bustling crowds, exchanging stories and sharing laughs as they peruse the wares on offer. I was particularly drawn to the stalls selling freshly caught fish, their displays piled high with shimmering specimens straight from the lake. Nearby, artisans showcase their talents, crafting intricate lacework and delicate glassware with skill and precision. As I wandered through the market, I was struck by the sense of history and tradition that infuses every corner, a reminder of the rich cultural heritage that defines this enchanting region.

- Boutique Shops

As a travel enthusiast who has explored the charming region of Lake Garda extensively, I'm excited to share my insights into the boutique shops scattered around this picturesque area.

Exploring the Boutique Shops

Now, let's delve into the world of boutique shopping in Lake Garda. From bustling promenades to hidden alleys, the region offers a diverse array of shops catering to every taste and preference. Whether you're hunting for designer fashion, artisanal crafts, or local delicacies, you're sure to find something that captures your imagination.

Fashion and Apparel

For fashion enthusiasts, Lake Garda boasts an impressive selection of boutique clothing stores showcasing the latest trends and timeless styles. In the elegant town of Sirmione, known for its thermal baths and medieval castle, you'll find boutique shops offering high-end Italian fashion brands, chic resort wear, and luxurious accessories. Stroll along the cobblestone streets and discover hidden gems tucked away in centuries-old buildings, where you can indulge in a shopping spree unlike any other.

In the picturesque town of Bardolino, famous for its vineyards and olive groves, boutique shops line the waterfront promenade, tempting visitors with a tempting array of clothing, footwear, and accessories. Whether you're searching for a stylish swimsuit, a breezy sundress, or a sophisticated ensemble for an evening out, you'll find plenty of options to suit your taste and budget.

Artisanal Crafts and Souvenirs

For those seeking one-of-a-kind souvenirs and artisanal crafts, Lake Garda offers a treasure trove of boutique shops showcasing the talents of local artisans. In the charming village of Malcesine, nestled at the foot of Monte Baldo, you'll find quaint boutiques selling handcrafted ceramics, intricate lacework, and colorful pottery inspired by the region's rich cultural heritage. Take a leisurely stroll through the narrow alleys and browse through the eclectic mix of shops, where each piece tells a story of tradition, craftsmanship, and creativity.

In the bustling town of Lazise, known for its medieval walls and picturesque harbor, boutique shops abound with unique souvenirs and keepsakes to remind you of your time by the lake. From hand-painted ornaments and artisanal chocolates to locally produced olive oil and fragrant lavender sachets, you'll find a diverse array of treasures to take home as mementos of your Lake Garda experience.

Gourmet Delights

No visit to Lake Garda would be complete without indulging in the region's culinary delights, and boutique shops offer the perfect opportunity to sample the flavors of the local cuisine. In the charming town of Garda, after which the lake is named, you'll find specialty food stores brimming with regional delicacies, including artisanal cheeses, freshly baked bread, and aromatic wines produced in the surrounding vineyards. Explore the quaint streets and alleys, and follow your nose to discover hidden gems where you can savor the authentic tastes of Lake Garda.

In the picturesque village of Limone sul Garda, renowned for its lemon groves and olive orchards, boutique shops tempt visitors with a tantalizing array of gourmet treats. From tangy citrus marmalades and fragrant olive oils to handmade chocolates and traditional pastries, you'll find an abundance of culinary delights to delight your taste buds and satisfy your cravings.

- Souvenirs and Handicrafts

As I stepped onto the shores of Lake Garda, I was immediately enveloped in the charm of its picturesque landscapes and vibrant culture. Amidst the breathtaking views of the azure waters and the majestic mountains, one aspect of Lake Garda stood out to me: its rich tradition of souvenirs and handicrafts.

Exploring the quaint towns and villages dotting the shores of Lake Garda, I quickly discovered a treasure trove of unique souvenirs and handmade crafts, each bearing the mark of the region's rich history and artistic heritage. From intricate lacework to exquisite ceramics, there was something to captivate every traveler's imagination.

One of the most iconic handicrafts of Lake Garda is its delicate lacework, which has been perfected by local artisans for generations. As I walked through the narrow streets of towns like Malcesine and Sirmione, I was drawn to the quaint boutiques showcasing intricate lace tablecloths, delicate handkerchiefs, and elegant clothing embellished with lace trimmings. Each piece told a story of meticulous craftsmanship and timeless elegance, making it the perfect memento of my visit to Lake Garda.

Another highlight of Lake Garda's artisanal scene is its vibrant ceramics industry. From hand-painted pottery to colorful tiles adorned with traditional motifs, the region's ceramic artisans create masterpieces that reflect the beauty of their surroundings. I found myself mesmerized by the dazzling array of ceramics on display in shops and markets, each piece a testament to the skill and creativity of its maker. Whether it was a handcrafted vase or a whimsical figurine, I knew that a piece of Lake Garda's ceramic art would add a touch of charm to my home.

As I delved deeper into Lake Garda's handicraft scene, I was delighted to discover a plethora of other treasures waiting to be uncovered. In the town of Limone sul Garda, I marveled at the intricate craftsmanship of the local olive wood carvers, whose skillful hands transformed humble pieces of wood into works of art. From intricately carved serving utensils to decorative ornaments, their creations showcased the natural beauty of the region's olive trees in all its glory.

Venturing further afield, I stumbled upon a bustling market in the town of Desenzano del Garda, where local artisans proudly displayed their wares. Here, I found myself surrounded by a dizzying array of handmade goods, from leather goods and jewelry to woven textiles and wooden toys. Each item bore the stamp of its creator's passion and creativity, offering a glimpse into the soul of Lake Garda's artisan community.

In addition to traditional handicrafts, Lake Garda also boasts a thriving culinary scene, with an abundance of local delicacies waiting to be savored. From fragrant olive oils and artisanal cheeses to delectable sweets like sbrisolona and torta di rose, the region's culinary offerings are as diverse as they are delicious. I made sure to stock up on some of these culinary delights to enjoy back home, knowing that each bite would transport me back to the shores of Lake Garda.

As I reflected on my journey through Lake Garda's world of souvenirs and handicrafts, I realized that these treasures were more than just material possessions—they were tangible reminders of the rich tapestry of history, culture, and artistry that defines this enchanting region. Whether it was a piece of lace, a ceramic vase, or a jar of olive oil, each souvenir told a story of the people and traditions that have shaped Lake Garda's identity over the centuries.

CHAPTER EIGHT

Practical Information

- Currency and Banking

As a seasoned traveler with a passion for exploring the hidden gems of Italy, Lake Garda holds a special place in my heart. Nestled amidst the picturesque landscape of northern Italy, Lake Garda beckons visitors with its shimmering waters, charming villages, and rich cultural heritage. In this comprehensive Lake Garda travel guide, I'll not only take you on a journey through the stunning sights and experiences this region has to offer but also delve into practical aspects such as currency and banking to ensure your trip is seamless and unforgettable.

Introduction to Lake Garda

Imagine waking up to the gentle rustle of olive groves and the soothing melody of lapping waves against the shore. That's the magic of Lake Garda. Located at the foothills of the Alps, this enchanting destination is Italy's largest lake, spanning three distinct provinces: Verona, Brescia, and Trentino. Its diverse landscape, ranging from serene lakeside towns to rugged mountainscapes, offers a plethora of experiences for every traveler.

Exploring the Currency

Before embarking on any journey, it's essential to familiarize yourself with the local currency. In Italy, the official currency is the Euro (EUR), denoted by the symbol €. One Euro is subdivided into 100 cents. Banknotes come in denominations of €5, €10, €20, €50, €100, €200, and €500, while coins are available in 1, 2, 5, 10, 20, and 50 cents, as well as €1 and €2.

Currency Exchange and Banking

Arriving in a foreign country often necessitates currency exchange, and Lake Garda is no exception. While airports and hotels may offer this service, they tend to levy higher fees and unfavorable exchange rates. For the best rates, it's advisable to exchange currency at local banks or authorized currency exchange offices, commonly found in town centers and tourist areas.

Alternatively, withdrawing cash from ATMs is a convenient option, provided your bank doesn't charge exorbitant foreign transaction fees. ATMs are widespread across Lake Garda, particularly in larger towns such as Desenzano del Garda, Sirmione, and Riva del Garda. Remember to inform your bank of your travel plans beforehand to avoid any potential card blocks due to suspicious activity.

Banking Services

Italian banks typically operate from Monday to Friday, with varying hours depending on the institution. Most banks are closed on weekends and public holidays, so it's advisable to plan any banking transactions accordingly. Major credit cards such as Visa, Mastercard, and American Express are widely accepted in tourist establishments, but smaller businesses may prefer cash payments.

For travelers requiring additional banking services, such as currency exchange, wire transfers, or traveler's checks, it's best to visit larger bank branches in urban centers like Verona or Brescia. English-speaking staff can assist with any inquiries or transactions, ensuring a smooth banking experience.

Navigating Lake Garda

Now that we've covered the practicalities of currency and banking, let's delve into the enchanting experiences awaiting you at Lake Garda. Whether you're a nature enthusiast, history buff, or simply seeking relaxation, there's something for everyone along the shores of this magnificent lake.

Exploring Lakeside Towns

One of the highlights of a visit to Lake Garda is exploring its charming lakeside towns, each with its own unique character and attractions. From the bustling promenades of Desenzano del Garda to the medieval alleys of Sirmione, these picturesque locales offer a glimpse into Italy's rich heritage and contemporary culture.

Desenzano del Garda, situated on the southwestern shore of the lake, is a vibrant hub known for its lively atmosphere and historic landmarks. Take a leisurely stroll along the waterfront promenade, lined with cafes, gelaterias, and boutique shops, or explore the imposing Scaliger Castle overlooking the harbor.

Further north lies Sirmione, renowned for its thermal baths and well-preserved Roman ruins. Be sure to visit the iconic Scaliger Castle, perched at the tip of the peninsula, and immerse yourself in the therapeutic waters of the Terme di Sirmione spa complex.

For a taste of traditional lakeside life, head to the charming town of Malcesine on the eastern shore. Its cobbled streets, medieval castle, and panoramic views from Monte Baldo make it a must-visit destination for history enthusiasts and outdoor adventurers alike.

Outdoor Adventures

With its idyllic landscape of azure waters and verdant hillsides, Lake Garda offers endless opportunities for outdoor recreation. Whether you're an avid hiker, cyclist, or water sports enthusiast, you'll find plenty of ways to immerse yourself in nature's beauty.

Hiking enthusiasts will delight in the scenic trails that crisscross the surrounding mountains, offering breathtaking views of the lake and beyond. The Monte Baldo range, accessible via cable car from Malcesine, boasts an extensive network of hiking paths suitable for all skill levels.

Cycling is another popular pastime around Lake Garda, with dedicated bike paths tracing the shoreline and meandering through quaint villages. Rent a bike and pedal your way along the picturesque Garda Bike Path, which spans over 140 kilometers from Limone sul Garda to Peschiera del Garda.

Water sports enthusiasts will find paradise on the lake's pristine waters, where windsurfing, sailing, and kiteboarding reign supreme. The northern town of Riva del Garda is particularly renowned for its favorable wind conditions, attracting windsurfers and sailors from around the world.

Culinary Delights

No trip to Lake Garda would be complete without savoring the flavors of its exquisite cuisine. From fresh seafood caught daily from the lake to regional specialties bursting with local ingredients, culinary enthusiasts will find themselves in gastronomic heaven.

Indulge in a leisurely lakeside lunch at one of the many waterfront trattorias, where you can savor freshly caught fish paired with a crisp glass of local wine. Be sure to try traditional dishes such as risotto al pesce persico (perch risotto) and polenta e luganega (polenta with sausage), showcasing the region's culinary heritage.

For a truly immersive experience, consider joining a cooking class or food tour led by local experts, where you can learn the secrets of Italian cuisine and sample artisanal products from nearby farms and vineyards.

Cultural Attractions

Beyond its natural beauty and culinary delights, Lake Garda is steeped in history and culture, with a wealth of attractions waiting to be discovered. From ancient Roman ruins to medieval castles, the region offers a fascinating glimpse into Italy's storied past.

History enthusiasts will relish a visit to the Grottoes of Catullus in Sirmione, one of the largest Roman villa complexes in northern Italy. Explore the ruins of this ancient seaside retreat, which dates back to the 1st century BCE, and marvel at its intricate mosaics and panoramic views of the lake.

Art aficionados won't want to miss a visit to the Vittoriale degli Italiani in Gardone Riviera, the former residence of poet and playwright Gabriele D'Annunzio. This sprawling estate is a testament to D'Annunzio's flamboyant personality, with its eclectic architecture, lush gardens, and museum showcasing his life and works.

For a glimpse into medieval history, venture inland to the town of Verona, renowned for its well-preserved Roman

- Language

One of the things that make Lake Garda so unique is its language. While Italian is the official language, the region has its own distinct dialect, known as

Gardesano. This dialect is a blend of Ita[lian,] German, and French, reflecting the area's hi[story] and cultural influences.

As you explore the towns and villages around the lake, you'll notice that many signs and menus are written in both Italian and Gardesano. While many locals speak some English, especially in the tourist areas, I always recommend learning a few key phrases in the local language. Not only is it a sign of respect, but it can also enhance your travel experience by allowing you to connect with the locals on a deeper level.

To help you get started, here are a few basic phrases in Gardesano:

* Buongiorno (Good day)
* Grazie (Thank you)
* Per favore (Please)
* Scusi (Excuse me)
* Mi dispiace (I'm sorry)

If you're interested in learning more about the language and culture of Lake Garda, there are plenty of resources available. One of my favorites is the Garda Trentino tourist information website, which offers a wealth of information on the region's history, traditions, and local products.

- Safety Tips

As a frequent traveler to Lake Garda, I've accumulated a wealth of knowledge about safety tips to ensure a smooth and enjoyable experience. Nestled in the picturesque region of northern Italy, Lake Garda is not only breathtakingly beautiful but also poses its own set of challenges and considerations for visitors. Whether you're planning a leisurely lakeside stroll, an adrenaline-fueled water sports adventure, or a scenic hike in the surrounding mountains, being prepared and informed about safety measures is paramount. Here's a comprehensive guide, from my perspective, to staying safe while exploring the wonders of Lake Garda.

Understanding the Risks

While Lake Garda's beauty is unparalleled, it's essential to recognize the potential risks associated with exploring this enchanting destination. From unpredictable weather patterns to water-related hazards, being aware of the dangers can significantly enhance your safety.

Weather Awareness

The weather around Lake Garda can be unpredictable, with sudden changes in temperature and occasional storms. Before embarking on any outdoor activity, check the weather forecast and plan accordingly. Carry appropriate clothing and gear to protect yourself from sudden rain or cold snaps, especially if you're hiking in the mountains or engaging in water sports.

Water Safety

As tempting as it may be to dive headfirst into Lake Garda's inviting waters, it's crucial to exercise caution, particularly if you're not a strong swimmer. Stick to designated swimming areas monitored by lifeguards, and never swim alone. Be mindful of underwater currents and always supervise children closely when they're near the water. If you're participating in water sports such as windsurfing or sailing, wear a properly fitted life jacket and familiarize yourself with local regulations and safety guidelines.

Boating Regulations

If you plan to explore Lake Garda by boat, familiarize yourself with the relevant regulations and safety procedures. Obtain the necessary permits and licenses, and ensure that your vessel is equipped with essential safety equipment such as life jackets, navigation lights, and a first aid kit. Respect speed limits and navigation rules, and always maintain a safe distance from other boats and swimmers.

Mountain Safety

The surrounding mountains offer spectacular hiking opportunities, but they also present potential hazards for the unprepared. Before setting out on a hike, research your chosen trail and assess your fitness level and experience. Carry a map, compass, and adequate supplies, including water, food, and a fully charged phone or GPS device. Dress in layers to accommodate changing weather conditions, and let someone know your itinerary before you depart.

Sun Protection

Lake Garda enjoys abundant sunshine, especially during the summer months, so it's essential to protect yourself from harmful UV rays. Wear sunscreen with a high SPF rating, sunglasses with UV protection, and a wide-brimmed hat to shield your face and neck. Seek shade during the hottest part of the day, typically between 10 a.m. and 4 p.m., and stay hydrated by drinking plenty of water.

Cultural Considerations

In addition to natural hazards, it's essential to be mindful of cultural norms and etiquette when visiting Lake Garda. Respect local customs and traditions, and familiarize yourself with basic Italian phrases to facilitate communication with residents. When dining out, observe table manners and tipping practices, and always greet people with a friendly "buongiorno" or "buonasera."

Emergency Preparedness

Despite our best efforts to stay safe, emergencies can still occur. Before traveling to Lake Garda, familiarize yourself with emergency contact numbers, including those for local police, medical services, and search and rescue teams. Carry a basic first aid kit with essentials such as bandages, antiseptic wipes, and pain relievers, and know how to administer basic first aid in case of minor injuries.

CHAPTER NINE

Accommodation Options

- Hotels

Choosing the Right Accommodation:

One of the first decisions you'll need to make when planning your trip to Lake Garda is selecting the perfect place to stay. Fortunately, the region boasts a wide array of accommodations, ranging from luxurious lakeside resorts to cozy bed and breakfasts. Here are a few options to consider:

1. Grand Hotel Fasano:

For those seeking a luxurious retreat, look no further than the Grand Hotel Fasano. Nestled on the shores of Lake Garda in Gardone Riviera, this elegant hotel exudes old-world charm and sophistication. With its spacious rooms, gourmet restaurants, and serene spa, it's the ideal choice for a pampering getaway.

2. Hotel Bella Riva:

Located in the enchanting town of Gardone Riviera, Hotel Bella Riva offers a boutique experience with personalized service and breathtaking views. Whether you're lounging by the infinity pool overlooking the lake or indulging in gourmet cuisine at the on-site restaurant, you'll feel like royalty during your stay.

3. Villa Cortine Palace Hotel:

For a truly unforgettable experience, consider staying at the Villa Cortine Palace Hotel in Sirmione. Set within a sprawling park overlooking the lake, this historic palace offers opulent accommodations, impeccable service, and unparalleled views. Relax in the lush gardens, take a dip in the infinity pool, or explore the charming town of Sirmione – the choice is yours.

Exploring the Surrounding Area:

Once you've settled into your accommodations, it's time to start exploring everything that Lake Garda has to offer. From leisurely boat rides to exhilarating outdoor adventures, there's no shortage of activities to enjoy.

1. Boat Tours:

One of the best ways to experience the beauty of Lake Garda is by taking a boat tour. Whether you opt for a guided excursion or rent a private boat, you'll have the opportunity to cruise along the crystal-clear waters, admiring the picturesque coastline and charming villages along the way.

2. Wine Tasting:

No visit to Lake Garda would be complete without sampling the region's world-renowned wines. Embark on a wine tasting tour to discover the rich flavors of local varietals such as Lugana and Bardolino, and learn about the winemaking traditions that have been passed down through generations.

3. Outdoor Adventures:

From hiking and cycling to windsurfing and sailing, Lake Garda offers a wealth of outdoor activities for adventure enthusiasts. Explore the rugged terrain of the surrounding mountains, paddle along the tranquil shores of the lake, or soar through the sky on a paragliding adventure – the possibilities are endless.

Sampling Local Cuisine:

No trip to Lake Garda would be complete without indulging in the region's delicious cuisine. From hearty pasta dishes to fresh seafood and decadent desserts, there's something to satisfy every palate.

1. Lakeside Dining:

For a truly unforgettable dining experience, head to one of the many lakeside restaurants scattered along the shores of Lake Garda. Enjoy freshly caught fish, locally sourced produce, and stunning views as you dine al fresco beneath the stars.

2. Traditional Trattorias:

For a taste of authentic Italian cuisine, be sure to visit one of the region's traditional trattorias. From hearty risottos to savory polentas, these cozy eateries serve up classic dishes bursting with flavor and made with love.

3. Gelato:

No trip to Italy would be complete without indulging in gelato, and Lake Garda is no exception. Treat yourself to a scoop (or two) of creamy gelato in an array of irresistible flavors – from classic favorites like pistachio and stracciatella to innovative creations like tiramisu and limoncello.

- Bed and Breakfasts

Exploring Lake Garda is a journey filled with hidden gems waiting to be discovered, and one of the best ways to immerse yourself in the local experience is by staying at a charming bed and breakfast. These intimate accommodations offer more than just a place to rest your head – they provide a glimpse into the heart and soul of the region, with personalized service, cozy rooms, and delicious homemade meals.

As I embarked on my Lake Garda adventure, I couldn't wait to discover the unique bed and breakfasts that dot the shoreline. From historic villas to rustic farmhouses, each property has its own story to tell and its own special charm.

My first stop is Villa Sostaga, a stunning 19th-century mansion nestled high above the lake. As I wind my way up the narrow mountain roads, I'm rewarded with sweeping views of the azure waters below. The villa's elegant facade and manicured gardens exude an air of sophistication, and I can't help but feel like I've stepped back in time.

Upon entering Villa Sostaga, I'm greeted warmly by the owners, who welcome me as if I were an old friend. The interior is tastefully decorated with antique furniture and classic artwork, giving the villa an air of old-world charm. My room, with its plush linens and panoramic lake views, feels like a luxurious retreat.

Each morning, I awake to the aroma of freshly brewed coffee and the sound of birdsong drifting through the open windows. Breakfast is a feast for the senses, with an array of homemade pastries, local cheeses, and freshly squeezed juices laid out on the sun-drenched terrace. As I sipped my espresso and savor each bite, I couldn't help but feel grateful for the simple pleasures of life at Villa Sostaga.

After breakfast, I set out to explore the surrounding countryside, taking leisurely walks through the vineyards and olive groves that carpet the hillsides. In the afternoon, I return to the villa to relax by the infinity pool, taking in the breathtaking views of the lake below. As the sun begins to set, I joined my fellow guests for aperitivo on the terrace, sipping local wines and swapping stories of our travels.

As my time at Villa Sostaga came to an end, I was reluctant to say goodbye to this slice of paradise. But Lake Garda has more treasures in store, and I'm eager to continue my journey.

Next, I made my way to La Casa degli Artisti, a charming bed and breakfast located in the historic town of Sirmione. Nestled amidst winding cobblestone streets and medieval architecture, this cozy inn is a hidden gem waiting to be discovered.

Upon arrival, I'm greeted by the owner, a talented artist who has transformed her home into a whimsical retreat filled with colorful paintings and quirky sculptures. Each room is uniquely decorated, with hand-painted murals and vintage furnishings adding to the charm.

I settled into my room, which overlooks a quaint courtyard filled with fragrant flowers and twinkling fairy lights. The atmosphere is enchanting, and I feel as though I've stepped into a storybook.

Each morning, I woke up to the sound of church bells ringing in the distance and the aroma of freshly baked pastries wafting through the air. Breakfast is a delightful affair, with a spread of homemade jams, crusty bread, and creamy cappuccinos laid out in the sunny breakfast room.

After breakfast, I spent my days exploring the historic streets of Sirmione, wandering through ancient ruins and medieval fortresses. In the evenings, I return to La Casa degli Artisti to unwind with a glass of wine in the cozy lounge, listening to the owner's tales of life in Lake Garda.

As my stay at La Casa degli Artisti came to an end, I'm filled with gratitude for the warm hospitality and unforgettable memories. Lake Garda has captured my heart, and I know that I'll return again someday to discover more of its hidden treasures.

My final stop on this Lake Garda adventure was Agriturismo Le Sorgive, a charming farmhouse nestled in the rolling hills of the Valpolicella wine region. Surrounded by vineyards and orchards, this rustic retreat offers a taste of rural Italian life in all its simplicity and beauty.

Upon arrival, I'm greeted by the owners, who welcome me with open arms and invite me to join them for a traditional Italian dinner. The farmhouse is cozy and inviting, with exposed wooden beams and stone walls adding to its rustic charm.

I settled into my room, which is decorated in a simple yet elegant style, with crisp white linens and views of the surrounding countryside. The peace and quiet are palpable, and I feel myself relaxing into the rhythm of agriturismo life.

Each morning, I work up to the sound of roosters crowing and the smell of freshly brewed coffee wafting through the air. Breakfast is a hearty affair, with farm-fresh eggs, homemade bread, and fruit picked straight from the orchard.

During the day, I explored the countryside on foot, hiking through vineyards and olive groves, and sampling the local wines and cheeses. In the evenings, I return to Agriturismo Le Sorgive to dine al fresco under the stars, savoring each bite of the delicious homemade cuisine.

As I bid farewell to Agriturismo Le Sorgive and Lake Garda, I'm filled with a sense of gratitude for the experiences I've had and the people I've met along the way. This magical corner of Italy has captured my heart, and I know that I'll carry its memories with me wherever I go. Until we meet again, Lake Garda, arrivederci. Ppl

- Campsites

As a seasoned traveler and avid camper, I've had the pleasure of experiencing some of the best campsites Lake Garda has to offer. From secluded spots nestled among olive groves to family-friendly resorts with all the amenities, there's something for every type of camper here. So, let me take you on a journey through the diverse array of campsites around Lake Garda, sharing my personal insights and recommendations along the way.

Choosing the Right Campsite:

When it comes to camping at Lake Garda, the options are endless. Whether you prefer a rustic tent pitch or a luxury glamping experience, there's a campsite to suit your needs and preferences. Here are some factors to consider when choosing the right campsite for your stay:

1. Location: Do you want to be close to the water, or would you prefer a more secluded spot in the mountains? Consider the proximity to the lake, as well as the surrounding attractions and activities you're interested in.

2. Facilities: Take a look at the facilities offered by each campsite, such as showers, toilets, laundry facilities, and recreational areas. If you're traveling with children, you may also want to look for campsites with playgrounds or entertainment programs.

3. Accommodation Options: Campsites around Lake Garda offer a variety of accommodation options, from traditional tent pitches to RV sites, cabins, and luxury safari tents. Choose the type of accommodation that best suits your needs and budget.

4. Reviews and Recommendations: Before making a decision, read reviews from other campers and check out recommendations from travel guides or websites. Pay attention to factors such as cleanliness, friendliness of staff, and overall atmosphere.

Now that you have a better idea of what to look for in a campsite, let's explore some of the best options around Lake Garda:

1. Camping Eden - San Felice del Benaco:

Nestled on the western shore of Lake Garda, Camping Eden offers breathtaking views of the lake and the surrounding mountains. The campsite features spacious tent pitches, as well as fully equipped bungalows and mobile homes for those seeking a more comfortable stay. Facilities include a swimming pool, restaurant, supermarket, and children's playground, making it ideal for families. The nearby town of Salò is just a short drive away, offering shops, restaurants, and cultural attractions to explore.

2. Camping Bella Italia - Peschiera del Garda:
Located near the southern tip of Lake Garda, Camping Bella Italia is one of the largest and most popular campsites in the area. With direct access to a private beach, as well as multiple swimming pools, sports facilities, and entertainment programs, there's never a dull moment at this lively resort. Accommodation options range from tent and RV pitches to chalets and apartments, catering to a wide range of budgets and preferences. The historic town of Peschiera del Garda is within walking distance, offering charming cafes, shops, and a picturesque harbor to explore.

3. Camping Du Parc - Lazise:
Situated on the eastern shore of Lake Garda, Camping Du Parc is a peaceful oasis surrounded by olive trees and vineyards. The campsite offers spacious pitches for tents and RVs, as well as comfortable bungalows and mobile homes with

modern amenities. Guests can enjoy access to a private beach, swimming pool, restaurant, and bar, as well as a range of recreational activities such as tennis, volleyball, and windsurfing. The charming town of Lazise is just a short stroll away, with its medieval walls, cobbled streets, and vibrant market square waiting to be explored.

4. Camping Spiaggia d'Oro - Lazise:
Boasting a prime lakefront location in the heart of Lazise, Camping Spiaggia d'Oro is a paradise for water lovers and sun seekers. The campsite offers spacious pitches with stunning views of the lake, as well as modern rental accommodations including bungalows, chalets, and apartments. Guests can relax on the private beach, take a dip in the swimming pool, or enjoy a meal at the on-site restaurant overlooking the water. The charming town center of Lazise is just a short walk away, offering shops, cafes, and gelaterias to tempt your taste buds.

5. Camping Butterfly - Peschiera del Garda:
Tucked away amidst lush greenery on the outskirts of Peschiera del Garda, Camping Butterfly is a peaceful retreat for nature lovers and outdoor enthusiasts. The campsite offers shaded tent pitches, as well as comfortable mobile homes and apartments for rent. Guests can relax by the swimming pool, play a game of tennis or volleyball, or explore the scenic walking and biking trails that surround the campsite. The vibrant town center of

Peschiera del Garda is within easy reach, offering shops, restaurants, and historic landmarks to discover.

- Rental Apartments and Villas

When it comes to choosing accommodation in Lake Garda, there are several factors to consider, including location, amenities, and budget. Whether you prefer the convenience of a centrally located apartment or the privacy of a secluded villa overlooking the lake, Lake Garda has something to suit every traveler's preferences.

Rental Apartments:
Renting an apartment is a popular choice for visitors to Lake Garda, especially for those looking for a comfortable and affordable accommodation option. From quaint studios to spacious penthouses, rental apartments come in a variety of sizes and styles, making them ideal for solo travelers, couples, families, and groups of friends alike.

One of the main advantages of staying in a rental apartment is the flexibility it offers. With a fully equipped kitchen and living area, guests have the freedom to cook their meals, relax in a home-like environment, and come and go as they please. This can be particularly appealing for travelers who prefer a more independent and self-catering experience during their stay.

In terms of location, rental apartments in Lake Garda can be found in various towns and villages surrounding the lake, each offering its own unique atmosphere and attractions. For those seeking a lively ambiance with plenty of restaurants, cafes, and shops, towns like Sirmione, Desenzano del Garda, and Garda are popular choices. On the other hand, if you prefer a quieter and more tranquil setting, villages like Malcesine, Limone sul Garda, and Torri del Benaco are worth considering.

When searching for a rental apartment in Lake Garda, it's essential to consider factors such as proximity to the lake, amenities, and parking availability. Many apartments offer stunning views of the lake and easy access to nearby beaches and waterfront promenades, allowing guests to make the most of their lakeside retreat.

Villas:
For travelers seeking a more luxurious and exclusive experience, renting a villa in Lake Garda is an excellent option. Villas offer privacy, space, and upscale amenities, making them ideal for

families, groups, or couples celebrating a special occasion.

One of the most significant advantages of staying in a villa is the opportunity to enjoy the ultimate in comfort and relaxation. With spacious living areas, private gardens or terraces, and often a swimming pool, villas provide a serene and idyllic setting where guests can unwind and recharge surrounded by breathtaking natural beauty.

In addition to luxurious amenities, many villas in Lake Garda boast stunning panoramic views of the lake and the surrounding mountains, creating a truly unforgettable backdrop for your stay. Whether you're enjoying a leisurely breakfast on the terrace, lounging by the pool, or watching the sunset over the water, the beauty of Lake Garda is always just a glance away.

When it comes to choosing a villa in Lake Garda, there are several options to consider, from historic mansions steeped in charm and character to modern, state-of-the-art properties with all the latest amenities. Some villas are located in secluded countryside settings, offering a peaceful retreat away from the hustle and bustle of the towns and villages, while others are situated within walking distance of local amenities and attractions.

Many villas in Lake Garda also come with additional services and amenities to enhance your stay, such as daily housekeeping, private chefs, and concierge services to help you plan activities and excursions during your visit. Whether you're looking for a romantic getaway, a family vacation, or a gathering of friends, renting a villa in Lake Garda allows you to create unforgettable memories in a truly spectacular setting.

CHAPTER TEN

Day Trips and Excursions

- Verona

As a traveler exploring the enchanting region of Lake Garda, Verona is an essential stop on your journey. Nestled on the banks of the Adige River, this historic city captivates visitors with its rich cultural heritage, stunning architecture, and romantic ambiance. Join me as we delve into the wonders of Verona, a must-visit destination on any Lake Garda travel itinerary.

Introduction to Verona

Stepping into Verona feels like stepping back in time. The city's illustrious past dates back over two millennia, with traces of its Roman, medieval, and Renaissance history visible at every turn. As you wander through its labyrinthine streets, you'll encounter ancient Roman ruins, majestic Renaissance palaces, and charming piazzas bustling with life. Verona's status as a UNESCO World Heritage Site speaks to its cultural significance and enduring allure.

Getting to Verona

Verona is conveniently located near Lake Garda, making it easily accessible for travelers. Whether you're arriving by car, train, or bus, reaching Verona is a straightforward journey. The city is served by Verona Villafranca Airport, which offers connections to major cities across Europe. From the airport, you can take a taxi or shuttle bus to reach the city center.

If you're traveling by train, Verona Porta Nuova is the main railway station, offering domestic and international services. From here, it's a short walk or bus ride to the heart of Verona. Alternatively, buses connect Verona to nearby towns and cities, providing another convenient option for travelers.

Exploring Verona

Once you've arrived in Verona, it's time to immerse yourself in all that this captivating city has to offer. Here are some highlights to include in your Verona itinerary:

1. Piazza delle Erbe: Start your exploration of Verona in the bustling Piazza delle Erbe, the city's vibrant central square. Lined with colorful buildings, lively cafes, and market stalls selling everything from fresh produce to souvenirs, this bustling piazza is the perfect place to soak up the atmosphere of Verona.

2. Juliet's House (Casa di Giulietta): No visit to Verona would be complete without a stop at Juliet's House, immortalized in William Shakespeare's timeless tragedy, "Romeo and Juliet." Though the balcony and courtyard are often crowded with tourists, the house's romantic allure is undeniable. Don't forget to rub Juliet's statue for good luck in love!

3. Verona Arena (Arena di Verona): Marvel at one of the best-preserved Roman amphitheaters in the world, the Verona Arena. Dating back to the 1st century AD, this ancient amphitheater once hosted gladiatorial contests and other spectacles. Today, it serves as a magnificent venue for opera performances, concerts, and other cultural events.

4. Castelvecchio: Explore the imposing Castelvecchio, a medieval fortress built in the 14th century by the powerful Scaliger dynasty. Wander through its formidable walls, admire the art collection housed within its galleries, and stroll across the iconic Castelvecchio Bridge, which spans the Adige River.

5. Piazza Bra: Relax and unwind in Piazza Bra, Verona's largest square and a popular gathering spot for locals and visitors alike. Admire the sweeping views of the Verona Arena, grab a gelato from one of the nearby cafes, and soak up the lively atmosphere of this bustling piazza.

6. San Zeno Maggiore: Discover the beauty of San Zeno Maggiore, one of Verona's most important churches and a masterpiece of Romanesque architecture. Admire the intricate bronze doors depicting biblical scenes, explore the interior adorned with stunning frescoes, and soak in the serene ambiance of this sacred space.

7. Scaliger Tombs (Arche Scaligere): Pay homage to Verona's medieval rulers at the Scaliger Tombs, a series of ornate Gothic mausoleums erected for the powerful Scaligeri family. Admire the intricate marble carvings and delicate details of these monumental tombs, which stand as testament to Verona's rich history.

8. Giardino Giusti: Escape the hustle and bustle of the city and wander through the peaceful oasis of Giardino Giusti. This beautifully landscaped Renaissance garden offers respite from the urban chaos, with manicured lawns, fragrant flower beds, and stunning panoramic views of Verona.

9. Ponte Pietra: Cross the ancient Ponte Pietra, Verona's oldest bridge spanning the Adige River. Dating back to Roman times, this picturesque bridge offers breathtaking views of the city skyline and serves as a timeless symbol of Verona's enduring beauty.

10. Wine Tasting: Indulge in Verona's rich culinary scene with a wine tasting experience in the nearby Valpolicella wine region. Sample exquisite wines such as Amarone and Valpolicella Classico, accompanied by delicious local cheeses and cured meats, and learn about the centuries-old winemaking traditions of the region.

Accommodation in Verona

Verona offers a wide range of accommodation options to suit every budget and preference. Whether you're looking for a luxurious hotel in the heart of the city or a cozy bed and breakfast tucked away in a quiet corner, Verona has something for everyone.

For those seeking luxury and sophistication, consider staying at one of Verona's upscale hotels, such as the iconic Due Torri Hotel or the elegant Hotel Gabbia d'Oro. These luxurious properties offer impeccable service, lavish amenities, and unparalleled views of Verona's historic landmarks.

If you prefer a more intimate and personalized experience, opt for a charming boutique hotel or bed and breakfast in Verona's historic center. These quaint accommodations exude charm and character, with cozy rooms, personalized service, and unique touches that will make your stay truly memorable.

For budget-conscious travelers, Verona also offers a variety of budget-friendly accommodation options, including hostels, guesthouses, and vacation rentals. These affordable properties provide comfortable accommodations at a fraction of the cost, allowing you to save money without sacrificing comfort or convenience.

Dining in Verona

No visit to Verona would be complete without indulging in the city's delectable culinary delights. Verona boasts a vibrant food scene, with an abundance of restaurants, trattorias, and osterias serving up traditional Venetian and regional cuisine.

Start your day with a leisurely breakfast at a charming cafe in Piazza delle Erbe, where you can savor freshly baked pastries, aromatic coffee, and panoramic views of the bustling square. For lunch, head to a local trattoria or osteria and sample classic dishes such as risotto al nero di seppia (squid ink risotto), baccalà mantecato (creamed cod), or polenta e osei (polenta with small birds).

In the evening, treat yourself to a memorable dining experience at one of Verona's top restaurants, where you can indulge in gourmet Italian cuisine paired with exquisite local wines. From cozy family-run eateries to Michelin-starred establishments, Verona offers a wealth of dining options to suit every palate and occasion.

Be sure to save room for dessert, as Verona is renowned for its delicious sweets and treats. Indulge in decadent desserts such as tiram

- Venice

Exploring Venice in Lake Garda is a unique experience that blends the charm of the Italian Riviera with the allure of one of Italy's most iconic cities. As a travel guide, I'll take you on a journey through this picturesque region, providing insights, tips, and recommendations to make the most of your visit.

Nestled in the northern part of Italy, Lake Garda is the largest lake in the country, renowned for its stunning landscapes, crystal-clear waters, and charming lakeside towns. With its mild climate, Mediterranean vegetation, and rich history, Lake Garda has been a popular destination for tourists seeking relaxation, outdoor activities, and cultural experiences.

Arriving in Lake Garda:

Your journey to Lake Garda typically begins with arrival at one of the nearby airports, such as Verona Airport or Milan Bergamo Airport. From there, you can easily reach the lake by car, bus, or train. As you approach Lake Garda, you'll be greeted by breathtaking views of the sparkling waters surrounded by rolling hills and picturesque villages.

Exploring Venice in Lake Garda:

One of the most fascinating aspects of Lake Garda is the presence of a charming town known as "Venice of Lake Garda." Located on the eastern shore of the lake, this town shares many similarities with its more famous counterpart, Venice. As you wander through its narrow streets and canals, you'll be transported to a world of Venetian-inspired architecture and ambiance.

Sights and Attractions:

- Canals and Bridges:Much like Venice, the town in Lake Garda features a network of canals lined with colorful buildings and crossed by charming bridges. Take a leisurely stroll along the waterfront promenade or hop on a boat tour to explore the town from a different perspective.

- Piazza San Marco: While smaller in scale compared to the iconic Piazza San Marco in Venice, this town's main square exudes a similar charm and vibrancy. Admire the elegant architecture of the surrounding buildings, relax at a sidewalk café, or simply soak in the atmosphere of this bustling hub.

- Churches and Palaces: Explore the town's historic churches and palaces, which showcase impressive architectural details and centuries of history. Don't miss the chance to visit the Church of San Giorgio or the Palazzo dei Capitani, both of which offer fascinating insights into the region's cultural heritage.

- Local Cuisine: Indulge in the delicious flavors of Venetian cuisine at one of the town's trattorias or osterias. From fresh seafood dishes to traditional risottos and polentas, you'll find plenty of culinary delights to tempt your taste buds. Be sure to pair your meal with a glass of locally produced wine for the perfect dining experience.

Activities and Excursions:

In addition to exploring the Venice of Lake Garda, there are plenty of activities and excursions to enjoy in the surrounding area:

- Boat Tours:Embark on a scenic boat tour of Lake Garda to discover its hidden coves, charming islands, and picturesque villages. Whether you opt for a leisurely cruise or an adrenaline-pumping speedboat ride, you're sure to be captivated by the beauty of the lake.

- Hiking and Cycling: Lace up your hiking boots or rent a bike to explore the scenic trails and pathways that wind their way around Lake Garda. From easy lakeside strolls to challenging mountain hikes, there's something for every level of outdoor enthusiast.

- Watersports:Dive into the crystal-clear waters of Lake Garda and try your hand at a variety of watersports, including sailing, windsurfing, kiteboarding, and kayaking. With its steady winds and calm waters, the lake is the perfect playground for water lovers.

- Wine Tasting:Venture into the surrounding countryside to discover the region's thriving wine industry. Visit local vineyards and wineries to sample a variety of wines, including the famous Bardolino and Lugana varieties, and learn about the winemaking process from knowledgeable experts.

Practical Tips for Visitors:

- Best Time to Visit: The best time to visit Lake Garda and Venice in Lake Garda is during the spring (April to June) and autumn (September to October) when the weather is mild, and the crowds are smaller.

- Accommodation:There are plenty of accommodation options available in the Venice of Lake Garda, ranging from luxury hotels and boutique guesthouses to cozy bed and breakfasts and self-catering apartments. Be sure to book your accommodation in advance, especially during the peak tourist season.

- Getting Around: The town in Lake Garda is easily navigable on foot, but if you want to explore the surrounding area, consider renting a car or using public transportation. Ferries and buses connect the town to other lakeside villages and attractions, making it convenient to explore the region.

- Respect Local Customs: Remember to respect the local customs and traditions during your visit to Lake Garda. Dress modestly when visiting churches and religious sites, and always greet locals with a friendly "buongiorno" or "buonasera."

- Safety Precautions:*While Lake Garda is generally a safe destination, it's always a good idea to take precautions to ensure a smooth and enjoyable trip. Keep your belongings secure, stay hydrated, and follow any safety guidelines provided by tour operators and local authorities.

Day Trips to the Dolomites:

While Lake Garda itself offers endless opportunities for exploration, no visit to the region would be complete without venturing into the nearby Dolomites. This UNESCO World Heritage site is renowned for its dramatic peaks, pristine alpine lakes, and scenic hiking trails.

One of the most popular day trips from Lake Garda is a visit to the charming town of Madonna di Campiglio, nestled in the heart of the Brenta Dolomites. Here, you can take a cable car ride to the top of Monte Spinale for panoramic views of the surrounding mountains, or explore the town's shops, cafes, and art galleries.

Another must-see destination in the Dolomites is the stunning Brenta Dolomites Nature Park, home to rugged peaks, lush forests, and cascading waterfalls. Hikers and nature enthusiasts will delight in the park's network of trails, which offer opportunities to spot wildlife such as deer, chamois, and marmots.

For a truly unforgettable experience, consider taking a scenic drive along the Great Dolomites Road, which winds its way through some of the region's most breathtaking landscapes. Along the way, you'll pass through charming mountain villages, cross towering mountain passes, and marvel at the sheer beauty of the Dolomites.

- Milan

As I stepped off the train in Milan, the bustling energy of the city enveloped me. I could feel the pulse of life vibrating through the streets, and I knew that my adventure in Lake Garda was about to begin. Milan, with its rich history, vibrant culture, and world-renowned fashion scene, served as the perfect starting point for my journey.

After exploring Milan's iconic landmarks such as the magnificent Duomo di Milano and the impressive Sforza Castle, I was ready to embark on the next leg of my trip to Lake Garda. I boarded a train bound for Desenzano del Garda, one of the major towns located on the southern shore of the lake. As the train chugged along, I couldn't help but feel a sense of anticipation building within me.

Upon arriving in Desenzano del Garda, I was greeted by the sight of crystal-clear waters stretching out before me, framed by picturesque villages and lush greenery. I immediately knew that Lake Garda was going to be nothing short of spectacular.

My first order of business was to find accommodations for my stay. Lake Garda offers a variety of options, from luxury resorts to cozy bed and breakfasts. After careful consideration, I decided to book a room at a charming lakeside hotel in the town of Sirmione. Situated on a narrow peninsula jutting out into the lake, Sirmione is known for its thermal baths and medieval castle, making it the perfect home base for exploring the area.

With my accommodations sorted, I set out to discover all that Lake Garda had to offer. From water sports such as sailing and windsurfing to leisurely boat cruises and scenic hikes, there was no shortage of activities to enjoy. I spent my days soaking up the sun on the lake's shores, taking in the breathtaking views of the surrounding mountains, and sampling delicious Italian cuisine at the local trattorias.

One of the highlights of my trip was visiting the town of Limone sul Garda, nestled on the lake's northwestern shore. Renowned for its lemon groves and quaint cobbled streets, Limone sul Garda exudes charm and tranquility. I spent hours wandering through the narrow alleyways, admiring the vibrant facades of the buildings and soaking in the laid-back atmosphere.

Another memorable experience was exploring the historic town of Malcesine, located on the eastern shore of Lake Garda. Dominated by the imposing Scaliger Castle, Malcesine is a haven for history buffs and culture enthusiasts alike. I climbed to the top of the castle's tower, where I was rewarded with panoramic views of the lake and surrounding countryside.

Of course, no visit to Lake Garda would be complete without indulging in some wine tasting. The region is known for its excellent wines, particularly the crisp whites and full-bodied reds produced in the vineyards that dot the landscape. I spent an afternoon sampling local varietals at a family-owned winery, learning about the winemaking process from grape to glass.

As my time at Lake Garda drew to a close, I found myself reluctant to leave this idyllic paradise behind. The beauty of the lake, the warmth of its people, and the richness of its culture had left an indelible mark on me. As I boarded the train back to Milan, I knew that Lake Garda would always hold a special place in my heart, and I vowed to return someday to experience its magic once again.

CHAPTER ELEVEN

Insider Tips and Recommendations

- Hidden Gems

Nestled in the northern part of Italy, Lake Garda is a haven of natural beauty, cultural heritage, and outdoor adventures. Surrounded by picturesque villages, vineyards, and olive groves, the lake offers a serene escape from the hustle and bustle of city life. Its crystal-clear waters are perfect for water sports enthusiasts, while its charming towns are a delight to explore.

Exploring Hidden Gems

1. Limone sul Garda

Our journey in Limone sul Garda, a quaint town with a rich history and stunning scenery. Tucked between the lake and the towering cliffs of the Monte Baldo range, Limone sul Garda exudes an old-world charm with its narrow cobblestone streets and pastel-colored buildings. Don't miss the

Limonaia del Castel, a unique lemon greenhouse dating back to the 18th century, where you can learn about the town's lemon-growing heritage.

2. Punta San Vigilio

For a secluded retreat, head to Punta San Vigilio, a peninsula on the eastern shore of Lake Garda. Surrounded by lush greenery and azure waters, this hidden gem is a favorite among locals for its tranquil ambiance and breathtaking views. Spend a leisurely day lounging on the pebble beach, exploring the botanical gardens, or dining at the historic Villa Guarienti.

3. Gargnano

Venture off the beaten path to discover Gargnano, a charming village nestled on the western shore of Lake Garda. With its medieval streets, Renaissance palaces, and waterfront promenade, Gargnano offers a glimpse into the region's rich history. Be sure to visit the San Francesco Church, known for its exquisite frescoes, and take a leisurely stroll along the Lungolago di Gargnano, where you can admire panoramic views of the lake.

4. Rocca di Manerba

For panoramic views of Lake Garda, make your way to Rocca di Manerba, a natural park located on a rocky promontory overlooking the southern shore.

Hike to the top of the hill to explore the ruins of a medieval fortress and soak in the sweeping vistas of the lake and surrounding countryside. The park is also home to rare plant species and offers opportunities for birdwatching and picnicking.

5. Monte Baldo

For outdoor enthusiasts, a visit to Monte Baldo is a must. This mountain range, often referred to as the "Garden of Europe," is renowned for its diverse flora and fauna, as well as its panoramic views of Lake Garda and the surrounding Alps. Take the Monte Baldo Cable Car from Malcesine to reach the summit, where you can embark on hiking trails, mountain biking routes, or simply enjoy a leisurely stroll amidst nature.

6. Bardolino

No trip to Lake Garda would be complete without a visit to Bardolino, a charming town renowned for its wine production and picturesque waterfront. Explore the narrow streets lined with shops, cafes, and gelaterias, or wander through the vineyards and olive groves that surround the town. Don't miss the opportunity to sample Bardolino's famous red wines, particularly the light and fruity Chiaretto rosé.

- Off-the-Beaten-Path Spots

Nestled in the heart of Northern Italy, Lake Garda is the largest lake in Italy, spanning three regions: Lombardy, Veneto, and Trentino-Alto Adige/Südtirol. Its crystal-clear waters are framed by majestic mountains, lush olive groves, and charming villages, making it a haven for nature lovers, adventure seekers, and culture enthusiasts alike.

Sirmione: Beyond the Crowds:

While Sirmione is undoubtedly one of Lake Garda's most popular destinations, there are hidden corners waiting to be discovered away from the crowds. Venture beyond the iconic Scaliger Castle to find secluded beaches like Jamaica Beach, where you can soak up the sun in peace or take a refreshing swim in the turquoise waters. Stroll through the narrow streets of the historic center to uncover quaint cafes, artisan shops, and local gems tucked away from the tourist hustle.

Monte Baldo: A Hiker's Paradise:

For those craving an adrenaline rush and panoramic views, Monte Baldo offers an escape into nature unlike any other. While many visitors opt for the cable car ride to the summit, adventurous souls can embark on the lesser-known hiking trails that crisscross the mountain. Follow the path less traveled to discover hidden waterfalls, alpine meadows adorned with wildflowers, and jaw-dropping vistas of Lake Garda below. Be sure to pack a picnic and savor the serenity of this alpine paradise.

Malcesine: Unveiling Hidden Charms:

Malcesine, with its medieval charm and cobbled streets, is a gem waiting to be explored beyond its picturesque harbor. Step off the main thoroughfare to discover hidden alleyways adorned with vibrant bougainvillea and ivy-clad facades. Explore the lesser-known churches and chapels, such as the Church of San Zeno, where you can admire exquisite frescoes and soak in the peaceful atmosphere away from the crowds. Don't miss the opportunity to dine at a local trattoria, where traditional flavors and warm hospitality await.

Limone sul Garda: Citrus Paradise:

Known for its lemon groves and Mediterranean climate, Limone sul Garda offers a slice of paradise away from the tourist crowds. Escape to the shores of the lake, where you can rent a kayak or paddleboard to explore hidden coves and secluded beaches. Wander through the town's maze of narrow streets to discover hidden gardens bursting with citrus trees, perfuming the air with their sweet fragrance. For a taste of local culture, visit the Limonaia del Castel, a restored lemon greenhouse where you can learn about the town's rich citrus-growing heritage.

Gardone Riviera: Art and Botanical Beauty:

While Gardone Riviera is renowned for the grandeur of the Vittoriale degli Italiani, Gabriele D'Annunzio's eccentric estate, there are lesser-known attractions waiting to be uncovered. Take a leisurely stroll through the Heller Garden, a botanical paradise showcasing a diverse collection of subtropical and Mediterranean plants. Discover hidden sculptures, tranquil ponds, and breathtaking views of the lake nestled amidst lush foliage. For art enthusiasts, a visit to the Andre Heller Foundation offers the opportunity to admire contemporary artworks in a serene lakeside setting.

Torri del Benaco: Tranquil Retreat:

Escape the crowds and immerse yourself in the tranquility of Torri del Benaco, a charming village steeped in history and natural beauty. Explore the ancient streets lined with stone houses adorned with colorful shutters, where time seems to stand still. Wander down to the lakeshore promenade to discover secluded spots where you can relax and take in the serene beauty of Lake Garda. Don't miss the opportunity to visit the Scaliger Castle, where you can admire panoramic views and immerse yourself in the town's rich maritime heritage.

.

- Budget-Friendly Activities

Exploring Lake Garda on a Budget:

1. Scenic Hiking Trails:
   - One of the best ways to experience the natural beauty of Lake Garda without spending a fortune is by exploring its scenic hiking trails. From gentle walks along the lake shore to challenging mountain treks, there's a trail for every level of fitness.
   - Monte Baldo, located on the eastern shore of the lake, offers breathtaking panoramic views accessible via a cable car ride from Malcesine. Once at the top, you can embark on various hiking routes, admiring the stunning vistas of Lake Garda and the surrounding mountains.

2. Cycling Adventures:
   - Renting a bike is an affordable and eco-friendly way to explore the picturesque villages and countryside around Lake Garda. Many towns offer bike rental services at reasonable prices, allowing

you to pedal along scenic cycling paths at your own pace.

- The Ciclopista del Sole, or "Sun Route," is a popular cycling trail that spans the length of Lake Garda, stretching from Limone sul Garda in the north to Peschiera del Garda in the south. This well-maintained route passes through vineyards, olive groves, and charming villages, offering a delightful journey for cyclists of all abilities.

3. Relaxing Beach Days:

- While Lake Garda may not have traditional sandy beaches, it boasts several designated bathing areas where visitors can soak up the sun and take a refreshing dip in the crystal-clear waters.

- The Spiaggia Baia delle Sirene in Garda is a picturesque pebble beach surrounded by lush Mediterranean vegetation, offering stunning views of the lake and the distant mountains. Entry to this public beach is usually free or requires a nominal fee, making it an affordable option for a day of relaxation.

4. Exploring Charming Towns:

- One of the joys of visiting Lake Garda is wandering through its charming lakeside towns, each with its own unique character and attractions. Stroll along cobblestone streets, admire historic architecture, and soak up the laid-back atmosphere without spending a dime.

- Sirmione, located on a narrow peninsula jutting into the southern end of Lake Garda, is particularly enchanting with its medieval castle, Roman ruins, and thermal baths. Take a leisurely walk around the town's picturesque streets or simply relax by the waterfront and enjoy the views.

5. Cultural Sightseeing:
   - Many cultural attractions around Lake Garda offer free or discounted admission on certain days of the week, allowing budget-conscious travelers to immerse themselves in the region's rich history and heritage without breaking the bank.
   - The Scaliger Castle in Malcesine, perched on a rocky promontory overlooking the lake, is a fascinating historical landmark dating back to the 13th century. While there may be a small entrance fee, the panoramic views from the castle's towers are well worth it.

6. Sampling Local Cuisine:
   - Enjoying delicious Italian cuisine doesn't have to be expensive, especially when dining at local trattorias and osterias that offer authentic dishes at affordable prices.
   - Try traditional Lake Garda specialties such as risotto al pesce, a creamy risotto made with locally caught fish, or polenta e osei, a hearty dish featuring polenta and small birds. Many restaurants also offer budget-friendly lunch specials or prix-fixe menus, allowing you to savor the flavors of the region without overspending.

7. Wine Tasting Tours:

- The Lake Garda region is renowned for its excellent wines, particularly the crisp white wines produced in the vineyards surrounding the lake. Many wineries welcome visitors for guided tours and tastings, providing an opportunity to sample world-class wines without breaking the bank.

- Look for smaller, family-owned wineries that offer personalized experiences and affordable tasting sessions. Some wineries may even waive the tasting fee with the purchase of a bottle of wine, allowing you to enjoy a memorable wine tasting experience without blowing your budget.

CHAPTER TWELE

Conclusion

As I conclude this comprehensive guide to Lake Garda, I find myself reminiscing about the mesmerizing beauty, rich history, and captivating experiences this enchanting destination has to offer. Nestled amidst the stunning landscapes of northern Italy, Lake Garda is a true gem that beckons travelers from around the globe to immerse themselves in its splendor.

Throughout this guide, we've explored the diverse array of activities and attractions that await visitors to Lake Garda. From the charming lakeside towns like Sirmione and Limone sul Garda, where history comes alive amidst medieval architecture and winding streets, to the breathtaking natural wonders such as the towering cliffs of Monte Baldo and the serene waters of the lake itself, there is no shortage of wonders to behold.

For outdoor enthusiasts, Lake Garda presents a playground like no other. Whether you're an avid hiker seeking panoramic views from high above the lake, a water sports enthusiast eager to windsurf or sail across its shimmering waters, or simply a leisurely stroller looking to soak in the tranquil ambiance of lakeside promenades, there's something here for everyone.

Culinary delights abound in the region surrounding Lake Garda, where fresh, locally sourced ingredients are transformed into delectable dishes that showcase the best of Italian cuisine. From traditional trattorias serving up homemade pastas and hearty risottos to upscale restaurants offering innovative takes on regional specialties, every meal is a feast for the senses.

But perhaps what sets Lake Garda apart most of all is its undeniable sense of tranquility and serenity. Whether you're savoring a glass of local wine as the sun dips below the horizon, exploring ancient ruins that whisper tales of centuries past, or simply unwinding amidst the beauty of nature, there's a palpable sense of peace that envelops you here, making it the perfect escape from the hustle and bustle of everyday life.

As I bid farewell to Lake Garda, I can't help but feel grateful for the memories made and the experiences shared in this idyllic corner of the world. Whether you're seeking adventure, relaxation, or simply a chance to reconnect with nature and yourself, Lake Garda offers it all and more. So pack your bags, embark on your own journey of discovery, and let the magic of Lake Garda captivate your heart and soul.

Printed in Great Britain
by Amazon